Cover's and inner pictures

created with the AI Dall- e

Translation by

Marta Carolina Martos Fernández

JESÚS Mª SILVA
CASTIGNANI

VIRGINITY

2.0

REGAIN INNOCENCE

Table of contents

Prologue..7

Introduction 10

Reading plan.......................................17

Day 1
The value of virginity....................20

Day 2
Losing virginity...............................34

Day 3
The power of faith........................55

Day 4
The importance of repentance.................62

Day 5
Recover virginity............................76

Day 6
The living water of the Spirit....................87

Day 7
Regenerated by the Holy Spirit................97

Day 8
Restored by God's merciful love............112

Day 9
Healing the consequences
of my mistakes...126

Day 10:
A look of wisdom on one´s own life......149

Day 11
Hand in hand with Mary and Joseph....169

Day 12
Workplan..177

This is for your partner
if has kept the virginity for you..............197

Prologue

Kiko Argüello once said that, in his beginnings, a gypsy woman interrupted one of the first meetings in which he announced the ´Kerigma´, to say that a relative of her died, and for as long as she did not see him resurrected, she would not believe. It is true that we Christians risk our credibility in resurrection. Nietzsche's challenge is known: he would not believe in Christians for as long as he did not see in them the face of the risen.

And it is indeed so: if Christ has not resurrected, our faith is futile, and we are the most miserable beings in the world. Had Jesus of Nazareth not resurrected, we would be just one more religion, one of many. Thus, the resurrection of Christ is not just a historical event that occurred twenty-one centuries ago; It is a historical fact that opens a new dimension to existence. Whoever associates with Christ participates of his resurrection, that is, He´s already resurrected to life with Him. Obviously, we are not talking about biological life, just as death is not only the interruption of the life of the body, but a force that´s continually active in our daily lives: «it manifests itself as suffering, disease, separation, rupture, the end of everything that is vital to us to the point of causing authentic "non-life" situations in which we are still alive biologically speaking»[1].

Father Silva believes in resurrection. He has the experience of dealing with the resurrected, and shouts in these pages to so many who suffer the force of "not feeling alive" in their hearts due to their past, for having lost their virginity. He wants them to stand before Christ and reminds them that the love of Christ is greater than their conscience, that they may just need to stretch their dry hand and regain life.

It takes courage: It does not remove death from what death means, and it does not remove life from what Life means. Since Christ resurrected, we know that life is stronger than death. Therefore, a second virginity is possible, it is possible to live the new life of Christ, in its fullness, whatever the situation and use made of it with our bodies so far.

This guide book is serious, demanding, hopeful, clear, concrete, entertaining, light ... This book will be a blessing to many. I just want to thank Father Jesus Maria who has detected this need of our world, and who has worked to contribute with this piece of writing.

José Pedro Manglano

---

1. ENZO BIANCHI, Una lucha por la vida, Sal Terrae, Santander 2012, p. 66.

Introduction

In the world we live in nowadays, many sexual taboos have been broken, and generally young people fool around with sensuality, and are initiated into the world of sexuality from a very early age. This makes a lot of people lose their virginity at a very young age, being unaware of what they are doing, the motives, and the consequences of these actions. It is not uncommon that, throughout your life, you end up regretting the things you have done when you were young.

I do not intend to analyze here the society we live in, nor show its mistakes. I do not write to face errors, but to encourage the practice of virtues. What moves me to write this book? In the first place, the love of Christ, which makes me love the Truth, and proclaim it without fear or shame. Second, my love for you, which makes me speak to you clearly about God's will for your lives, for your body and soul. And thirdly, the love of chastity, which makes me propose this path for your own lives with simplicity. Because I am firmly persuaded that the Lord wants the best for all of us. If He calls us to chastity, it is without a doubt because this virtue is in the way of our happiness, for the fullness of our souls.

However, I am aware that living chastity today is not easy; and what's more, it can be a lot more difficult than in other times of history. When Christianity came into contact with the Greek and Roman world, upon detaching from the Jewish society, they encountered a society driven by lust, which exalted sexual vice as a virtue, and practiced it without complexes or taboos. Thanks to Christianity, the importance of the virtue of chastity was extended, to the point of falling into excessive puritanism.

Since the world has gradually moved away from religion, and specifically from "sexual revolution onwards, "the esteem for chastity" was lost again. Our society closely resembles that of ancient Greek and Roman culture; with regards to sex. Therefore, young Christians find themselves in an environment where sexual initiation is very easy, fast and early. Pornography, masturbation and sexual relations of all kinds are easy, sudden, and fleeting. Very easily, before you even know it, you are entangled in all those issues, thus losing your purity and innocence very quickly. This is a fact nowadays.

However, my intention when writing this book is not to change society - hopefully it will change soon though. The purpose of this book is for the young Christians who have been hurt, and have lost their virginity in the fast path of life:

I know young Christians who, having clarity about their desire to live chastity, in a moment of negligence and weakness they've had sex and they lost their virginity.

I know young people who have lost their virginity and later on they have converted to Christianity. When they discovered the virtue of chastity and the importance of virginity, it was already late for them in that sense, because they had sex.

I know young Christians who never heard about the virtue of chastity, and who do not live that virtue because they do not consider it a consequence of their faith.

I know young Christians who keep chastity in a warm parenthesis, and who have not yet decided whether or not they will remain virgin until marriage, waiting to see where the circumstances of life drift them to.

I know young Christians who want to stay virgin until marriage, but who are not so clear about whether other sexual actions, other than going all the way, sexually, may be right, or not, or whether that may have negative consequences for them or their relationship.

I know young Christians who want to experience the virtue of chastity, but they begin to date another person who is not clear about this issue, and finally they end up giving in and having sex with them, feeling a pressure on their part, directly or indirectly.

I have talked to lots of young people about the reasons for living chastity and virginity, and many of you have understood and accepted them; but later, when you have started a serious relationship with someone, you have experienced in your own skin the difficulties of living by that decision, and you have ended up gradually giving in to the desires of the flesh, to the point of getting to lose your virginity. This did not happen due to ill intention or driven by lust; or at least, not just driven by lust.

This happens due to loving the other person, the natural dynamics of love that lead to an increasingly intimate surrender; driven by a desire of melting with the other person, often born at the wounds of childhood and adolescence; and also due to the ease of access to the world of sexuality in our hyper-erotic world...

This book is addressed to all those people who after having sex, have decided to live chastity.

To those of you, who after losing your virginity, have discovered God's will for your lives, and want to live by it.

To those of you, who, perhaps, would have preserved your virginity to give it to the man or woman of your life.

To those of you, who would like to offer to God or to your future husband or wife the gift of your virginity, but you feel you can no longer do that because you have already lost it.

To those of you, who do not know very well how you would like to live love, and to those who, knowing it, they still don´t know whether they will be able to live love in chastity.

To those of you, young people, who have decided to surrender to the Lord in the priestly or consecrated life. More and more young people receive this vocation after losing their virginity. All that is said here will also be worth reading in order to recover it, so that you can then surrender yourselves to the Lord with a virgin heart. Whatever it´s said here concerning the surrender to a husband or wife, you can apply it perfectly to your surrender to God.

I want to help all of you in this process of recovering your virginity. Do you think it is impossible? «It is impossible for men, but not for God; God is almighty» (Mt 19, 26).

Reading plan

This is not a book to be read quickly and all at once. It is a deep book that aims to transform your soul. Therefore, I propose that you read one chapter per day, meditating it quietly and slowly. This way, what you read will go into your heart, and you will have the time to let it sink in. You will be able to go back to what you have read several times in the day, and you will not tiptoe through a book that can change your life and give you a new heart.

As you read on, you will find practical suggestions, prayers and concrete things you can do; This is how the progressive path of regeneration that this book offers you will take place.

In the last chapter of the book, I will offer you a very concrete pathway, a work plan, which I invite you to follow step by step, so that you can seal the virginity back into your heart again.

Perhaps, when you get to the last chapter of the book it may help you to go back to the beginning and read it again, faster this time round, before starting that work plan. That way everything you are going to read here will sink in deeper in your heart and make it easier for you to start a new life. Having said that, you may do what you feel is going to help you the most. In the end, we all travel by ourselves, and you may know better than anyone what method suits you best.

Read the whole book! Nowadays we have no time for anything, let alone to read. Not a few young people have started reading this book, but they have left it halfway through because they didn't have time. Don´t make that mistake; there will be parts that will require more effort of you to go through, and parts that you feel less identified with. Trust me: read it all. If you do, you'll thank me.

Read slowly!

I know that today we are used to reading little and fast. This book is easy to read in the sense that it´s language is easy; But don't be fooled by that. It is a profound book that can cause a huge change in you and a great regeneration in your heart, which may be decisive for the rest of your life. Read it well, slowly, understanding and meditating; if you don´t, it will only serve you halfway. Why? Because we must let things rest in the heart, and from there the grace of the Holy Spirit will transform our lives. Our nature has its processes and things take their time. So, read slowly, enjoy, pray and meditate, and you will experience how the grace of the Holy Spirit gives you back the virginity and innocence of the soul that you may have lost.

Day 1

The value of virginity

I think it is important to start by briefly pointing out the value of chastity and virginity. Why? Because it wouldn´t make sense to want to recover something that we do not know what it is, or the motivation for it.

Chastity is a virtue by which I master my sexual abilities to put them at the service of love. It is a virtue, which means, it requires a personal effort, and it also requires the grace of God. Through chastity I own myself, and I do not become a slave of my passions, for it is I who manage my capacity for the sexual, and I do not let sexuality drag me.

God has given me a sexual capacity, not to fiddle with it, but for me to integrate it into my personality and preserve it, until the time comes, when I will become one flesh with the person whom I choose to love for the rest of my life.

Jesus, who has come to teach us who we really are, tells us that the union of spouses has a much more beautiful and deeper meaning than that given by today's world. That is why the Lord says in the Gospel: «Have you not read that the Creator, from the beginning, created them man and woman, and said: "Wherefore a man shall leave father and mother, and shall cleave to his wife: and they shall be two in one flesh" (Gn 2, 24). For what God has united, may not be separated by man» (Mt 19, 4-6). When Jesus says that they become "one flesh," he is saying that it is a total and forever union, which gives birth to a new reality formed by the two spouses.

It is clear that the world in which we live would not agree on this. On the contrary, it makes us believe that sex is reduced to playing with my body and other people´s, without further implications or consequences.

Faced with this, we shall bear in mind that our bodies are not a part of us: it is us. When I give myself away, my body, I give away my own heart. And my heart is prepared to fully and exclusively love only one person, for a lifetime; and for me to give myself totally, sexually, to that person, and be "one flesh" with them, and thus give birth to a new life, to a family. Like God himself, who in his eternity is a communion of people who give themselves to each other; like the love of God, which overflows, giving birth to other creatures that He also loves. It is superb that God calls man to imitate Him! It is a wonder that human love is an imitation of the very being of God!

Sexuality is something beautiful, very high, and when you live it in accordance with the will of God, it is a source of holiness and happiness for those who experiment it. It is not true that for the

Church "sex is bad," or that, as they say today, "everything that provides pleasure, either makes you fat or it´s a sin." Not true! God has created us sexed and sexual, capable of giving ourselves to another in body and soul, in an act full of pleasure that unites us totally and emotionally to the other person. This is how God wanted it! And what God wants for us is always something good: «God saw everything he had created, and it was very good» (Gn 1, 31). Also sex. Indeed, in the Creation story the Lord says that «it is not good for the man to be alone» (Gn 2, 18). And just after that he presents us with that complementarity between man and woman who give themselves up and form a single flesh. All this is good. However, the biblical text says one very surprising thing immediately after: «They were both naked, the man and his wife, but were not ashamed of each other» (Gn 2, 25.). What does that refer to? It is obvious! It means that men and women could look at each other with purity, with chastity. In his initial plan, God wanted man and woman to give themselves up to each other with love, to form one flesh and give birth to new life, in a total union full of pleasure. There was no lustful desire, no desire for domination, no need for fusion.

Only when the man and the woman turned away from the will of God and used their gifts for something which He had not destined them for, mess was introduced. In fact, after sin, the biblical text says that «they both opened their eyes, and realized that they were naked; and intertwining fig leaves, they were girdled (Gn 3, 7)». They had lost the ability to look naked without igniting disorderly desires. That is why they had to hide their private parts, because their gaze was no longer innocent. From this first disorder, an even greater one was introduced in the relations between man and woman, which the Lord points to the woman when he explains the consequences of her sin: «You will crave your husband, and he will dominate you (Gn 3, 16)». It is important that we do not understand this text referring only to women, since the desire to dominate, to possess the other, to reduce it to one's own will, affects both men and women.

Let us notice that the Lord does not speak of lust; even when this union between man and woman is made for love and with love, it can be messy. It is from the fall into sin that the virtue of chastity becomes necessary.

There is a precious detail of the biblical text. After sin, the first men made fig-tree girdles for themselves – made of vegetables and scrapes, as if they were a penance. But «the Lord God made for the man and his wife animal skin robes and clothed them» (Gn 3, 21).

In this way, the Lord confirmed the first men in goodness and the need for modesty and chastity; but not as a penance, but as a virtue; not with loincloths of leaves, but with skin robes, a sign of the sacred dignity of their bodies that, from then on, they'd had to take care of with shame, so that it served the purpose for which He had created the body.

As the gaze of man and woman became obscured by sin, it is no longer easy to live the relationship with the other with purity, knowing how to wait, not wanting to dominate, not wanting to impose one's will, not wanting to satisfy one's passion above of everything else... Now a virtuous effort is necessary, so that my impulses are at the service of love and surrender; Now it is necessary to strive to be free, so that my will commands me and not passion. And this is an admirable struggle, in which true respect is played towards the person I love, in which I can show them that I truly love them, and that I want to love them well.

Chastity, therefore, is not a slab or a repression; It is a struggle for freedom and the purity of love, for respect for the other and for building the future on the solid basis of a free and total love.

Jesus calls us to chastity, not because he wants to take something good from us, but because he wants us to live it well, so that it helps us to be happier. Our heart desires to give itself up, it has been created for that. But before fulfilling our heart's gift of donation, the Lord teaches us that there is a commitment, a sacrament, that must precede this surrender and that ensures it: marriage.

Marriage is a commitment by which I swear to love the other person always and in all circumstances; I swear to love that person and only them. The marriage must precede sexual surrender; First I give myself to you with all my heart and I swear to love you faithfully for a lifetime, and then I seal that commitment by giving myself to you sexually, with all my being, body and soul. This is the order and meaning that the Lord wanted, by making us capable of committing and giving ourselves to each other. For this he has endowed us with those capabilities, and he calls us to it. And even if today's world doesn't see it that way, this is what the Lord has transmitted to us.

Why? Because He loves us; and as he loves us, he shows us the path of our own fullness. Because many times - even with good will - we can go wrong along the way.

And those mistakes have consequences. That is why Saint Paul says: «For I do not do the good that I desire, but I do the evil that I do not want» (Rm 7, 19).

Because of the confusion that sometimes exists between our good desires and our passions, the Lord shows us the way for us to live well the desire for sexual surrender in our hearts: chastity and virginity until marriage. And when we hear that the Lord calls us to chastity and virginity, what St. Paul tells us also remains true: «I tell you all this for your good; not to set you up, but to induce you to a noble thing and to deal with the Lord without worries» (1 Cor 7, 35). If the Lord loves you, and you love the Lord, trust Him. How will he ask you for something that is bad for you or makes you unhappy? He knows what he created you for. He has given you sexuality so that you live it at the right time and in the right way. If you live it like that, it will be a source of fullness for you, because God has given it to you for your happiness. But if you don't live it like that, you turn sexuality into something that, instead of humanizing you, dehumanizes you.

And this does not only refer to complete sexual relations... If the Lord has created us with sexual capacity not to fiddle with it, but for absolute devotion, then every use of sexuality that is not at the service of love donation only, does not make sense either:

- Pornography animalizes us, brings out the worst in us and deceives us. It shows us irrational scenes, often full of violence and dominance. It presents women willing to do anything or letting someone do anything to them. It unrealistically increases our sexual expectations. It induces us to understand sex as something separate from love and as an object of consumption. It makes us unfit for fidelity. And a long etcetera that each one of us could deduce.

- Masturbation is a selfish use of sexual abilities that is accompanied by pornography, or dirty thoughts about other people. It creates in us a habit that makes it very difficult for us to understand and live sex as an act of donation, because it makes us used to live it in a selfish way, as a search for individual pleasure. Not a few people whom I have received in confession have experienced it as an authentic infidelity.

In addition, learning to have self-control will help me cope with different situations in life. During the marriage there will be times when it is necessary to space sexual relations for several reasons; if I am not able to master my sexual instincts, if I do not own myself because of the virtue of chastity, in those times it could be very difficult for me to be faithful to my husband or wife. I may flirt, fall into dangerous friendships, search for affective or material compensation, masturbation, demands upon my husband or wife, temper and anger at home, infidelity, prostitution, etc.

Chastity is not dark or repressive, but bright, because it enables me to be faithful, to own myself, to be free. With my freedom I can integrate all my emotional and sexual capacities and make them serve my vocation, my decision to love the person with whom I will share the rest of my life...

LET´S RECAP...

Chastity does not begin in courtship, but much earlier. It is like a training that, since adolescence, is preparing me so that the total dedication I will live in marriage is a source of satisfaction, and not of frustration. And that means not letting myself be dragged by what I don't want to live: flirting, pornography, masturbation, infidelity, sex, etc..

Chastity makes me free, strong, sacrificed, bright.

Chastity makes me mature and capable.

Chastity helps me to be myself, not to be a slave.

Chastity is the best cover letter for the person I love.

Let them laugh at me! Let them make fun, try to convince me! Tell me that I am going against the tide, that I don't know what I am missing! What do I care?

I know what I want, and I know what I am willing to fight to get there.

I know what I am willing to give up for a love so precious, so perfect.

I know it won't be easy, and that there will be falls, temptations, dark moments and difficulties along the way.

I am not going to let anything or anyone obscure the ideal that Jesus Christ has lit in my heart.

And the day I give myself up to my wife - or my husband - with a faithful, total, free and pure love, the satisfaction I will live will more than compensate for all the effort and all the sacrifices, because I will have become a man of integrity, a woman of integrity, according to God´s heart.

Day 2

Losing virginity

After showing the ideal to which the Lord calls us, we enter into the subject at hand. And what about those who have lost their virginity? What about those who have not lived up to that ideal, for one reason or another?

"Losing" virginity is a strong statement. It refers to a very concrete fact, very real, that happens at a given time, the "first" time, and it marks before and after "that event" in our life.

In our society, even having left all sexual taboos behind, people keep talking about losing virginity. Although it is presented as something good, something desirable and something you should do as soon as possible, the idea of loss remains. From the Christian perspective it is a beautiful thing to lose virginity with the person that has been chosen and with whom one has engaged in marriage; It is a precious wedding gift. However, many of you - maybe the majority of you - will arrive at your wedding night without that seal.

You may have lost your virginity by a slip, or before you decided to embrace chastity; or for being with someone you loved very much and who you thought would be the one; or because in adolescence you let yourself get carried away by passion or curiosity, and you became entangled; or because you were presented with the opportunity and you didn't want to let it slip; or because they told you many times that you didn't know what you were missing and didn't want to wait anymore to find out; There could be so many reasons, that may have led you to have sex... And not always with malice or lust, nor with a desire for exploitation; sometimes with naivety, or out of curiosity, or even out of love; for the confusion planted in your heart by sexual forces, social and group pressure, by the fall of the barriers of modesty, etc. Whatever it was that led you to lose your virginity, you did it. And that is not going to change.

I once confessed a teenager that during a party he got drunk enough and smoked marijuana. In that state, a girl took him, and slept with him. He wanted to remain a virgin until marriage, but all his barriers had fallen and he was dragged into it. The next morning he didn't remember anything that happened; I just knew he had. He came to me in pain, bewildered, and said: "Father, my virginity has been stolen." He was a good boy, but circumstances gently pushed him to do something he did not really want to do. The gravity with which he came to me, his face ... made me realize how precious virginity is, and how easy it is for one to "be robbed." Maybe you feel that way too; Maybe you somehow feel that your virginity has been stolen; you may not even remember, or at that time you were not fully aware of what you were doing...

Do not worry! I have written this book precisely so that you realize that you have not done anything that cannot be repaired. If your virginity has been stolen, the Lord will give it back to you.

I remember a boy who, as a teenager, was looking forward to having sex.

Everyone does it, I don´t want to be the last one! He was quite entangled in porn and masturbation, and we can say that, because of his environment, the idea of having sex burned inside. The occasion came when he fell madly in love with a girl who sexually gave him everything he wanted. They went out for many years, and the boy ended up discovering that she was cheating on him with another guy; She made him believe that she loved him, but actually she was only using him. This generated a lot of resentment in him. Years later he converted, and upon discovering the value of chastity, he also discovered the damage that his relations with that girl had caused him. He decided to live chastity, asked the Lord for a new virginity, and God granted it ... through this book. Is this your case? Then go ahead! God is going to give you a new understanding of love, and it will give you back your lost virginity.

A girl whom I accompanied spiritually was very much in love with her boyfriend. They both had a very clear mind of what they wanted and did not want to do to in their relationship. At some point, the two were convinced that they were made for each other and that their love would last a lifetime; they knew they were going to get married. He began to change his thinking on the subject of sexuality:

«Let's see, if we love each other so much, if we are sure that we are made for each other, if we want to get married, and we don't do it yet just because we are young and we have no means, why not have sex? Our relationship demands a step further, it is only about advancing the moment. If we are so clear that we will always be together, why wait?» She did not know what to do. On the one hand she loved him very much; he was trying to go further, and she wanted it too, of course. But on the other hand, she knew that God was calling her to live marriage in chastity. Finally, she finally gave in and convinced herself of what her boyfriend was saying, and they began having a sexual relationship. Things went well. But after a year she told me that her boyfriend had changed a lot, that she didn't recognize him and that she didn't know what to do. After a while, they finished. She came to me feeling very down. «A year ago I was convinced that he was the man of my life, the only one I was going to have sex with and I was wrong». That's where she discovered the reason for keeping virginity until marriage; That moment, she understood why it is necessary to celebrate the commitment of marriage, by which they both have to swear that they will always remain united, before being able to seal that union with the surrender of the body itself. If that commitment is not given - because I am not yet old enough, because I have not finished my degree, etc. - I am not prepared to have sex. If your case is similar to this, don't worry! God is going to work a miracle in you and will give you a new heart so that this time round you will give your virginity to the man or woman of your life.

A boy who bounced from Church began to "have fun", living a crazy life. He was very attractive and was very stylish, so it wasn´t difficult for him to seduce girls and have sex with them. There came a point where he was having sex with several girls at the same time, and he told them that it was a condition. I they didn't like that, they would look for another guy... several years later, he began to experiment an emptiness in his heart, and that emptiness prompted him to approach the Church, where he had an experience of God that "Threw him off his horse", like St. Paul´s. He experimented a radical conversion, and in the light of God's love, he realized how he had depraved his own body and that of others, hurting the Lord and the Virgin Mary. He repented profoundly of what he had done, he confessed, and met with the girls he had sex with, one by one, to tell them what had happened to him in his conversion and apologized. Some of them pulled his leg, others thought he lost his mind; but most of them were impressed by that gesture — and some even, approached the Church thanks to him. He began to live a life of chastity, and God restored his heart. And he can do the same with yours! As Jesus says, just have faith.

We cannot change the past. It happened and that´s it. We've all wanted to travel backwards to change the decisions we made one day. That is repentance, in part. But we go there using our imagination, because in reality it isn´t possible. Therefore, recovering virginity is not restoring what happened; that's impossible. And the memory of what happened will always be, more or less vivid, but it will definitely remain.

So, is virginity something that we lose and cannot be recovered? What solution do we have left?

Not few people of those who lost their virginity and then started a Christian life, do live with resignation about it: «Well, done that now, there´s no point crying over spilt milk". No point going over it in my head. It may not be so important, after all. I will look for the good side, and move on». Some young man, determined to start living chastity after having lost his virginity, even told me: «No one can steal the fun I had from me». These types of affirmations are typical of young hearts that seek to continue with their lives as if nothing happened, trying to minimize the consequences of their actions, because they know they can no longer change them. We all feel like that when we make a mistake. What happens with that attitude is that it prevents a deep and complete regret from taking place.

But then, what are we supposed to do? Get stuck pitifully in the past? Lick your wounds? Spend all day lamenting for the mistakes made and never move on? Keep reminding myself of what I´ve done wrong? Of course not!

Once, a woman came in anguish to talk to me. After having been happily married for years, she said that while making love with her husband, she suddenly remembered another guy with whom she had a sexual relationship in the past. That made her feel very bad, she didn't understand why this happened. It was not that she didn´t love her husband, nor that she enjoyed the other guy more, but she couldn´t help that thought slipping through her, and she was distressed. And she told me: "Now I understand why the

Church tells us that we have to keep virginity till marriage." I told her not to worry, it was normal to remember those past experiences, because the past is what it is. That didn't mean she didn't love her husband, but that she had to heal her memories and close those wounds that were still open. And in a very beautiful process, she was able to heal those issues and live her relationship in a renewed way. She was not trapped in her past, nor simply turned the page, resigned. The Lord healed her heart.

I remember another case of a guy who, after having lived a sexually disorderly life, he was determined to live in chastity and began to be distressed at the fact that he had lost his virginity: «What if I am not able now to have loving sexual relationships with love, giving myself to the other? What if my selfishness slips? What if I don't know how to love my future wife? And if it is not sexually the same as it was with the others? What if...?" I told him two things: first, that God was calling him to live the present, and that at every moment He would give him the grace he needed to live things well. And secondly, that God could heal his heart and restore his virginity, and that what he would live with his future wife would be very different from what he had lived so far. So it was. God is powerful and good! "What if..." comes from devil. God takes care of our past, present and future. God calls us not to fear. As Father Joseph Kentenich said: "God comes every day for every day".

The enemy of human nature will always lead us to one of these two attitudes: turn the page too fast, downplaying our error, or remain distressed, letting our sin do our head in. Both options are wrong. Why? Because they don't leave opportunity for the Lord to restore and regenerate our hearts. Both put myself at the center, and with the conclusion that there is nothing I can do to feel different. Both deny the power of God over my life and my heart.

I am not talking about forgiveness here. Of course, God can forgive our sins through confession, which is a sacrament of relief for those who fall. Through confession, our sins are destroyed and the grace of Holiness is returned. Without that forgiveness received in confession, it is impossible to recover virginity. But that is not enough. There is something much greater than the power of God can work in our lives: restore my virginity and regenerate my heart.

The world around us offers us a biased look at love and sexuality. It seems that nothing is forever, that sex is on one side and love is on the other. Many times marriage is not presented as a beautiful and desirable path, but as a residue of an earlier era, of a traditional culture; as something old fashioned and called to disappear. You may not think like that, but you can´t deny that the world in which you live affects you, and that - perhaps - having had sex has made you forget the value of marriage, or not give it the importance it has. I remember an occasion when, walking down the street, I saw a boy wearing a shirt that said: «Sex is the price women pay for marriage. Marriage is the price that men pay for sex». I refuse to resign myself to accept that! I claim the value of the beauty of love, commitment, and sacrifice!

What have you been created for? What is the deepest desire that God has inscribed in your heart? The desire to love and be loved. But love is not just a feeling, it is much more. Love may almost always begin with an emotion that moves me to approach and meet a person; but once I know them, my intelligence activates and enlightens me to go further, deeper, so that my heart feels more and more affection for that person; an affection that finally moves me to decide for her, to start a serious relationship, which is gradually growing in involvement and commitment, in a virtuous circle that leads to the decision to share a lifetime. In this way, we see that true love arises when the whole person is involved: emotion, intelligence and will. Therefore, love is more than a feeling. All the dynamics of love are concentrated on a decision. What decision? Give myself to the other person. Love is delivery.

This is the greatest beauty to which any man or woman can aspire. God has created us for love; we come to life through an act of love of our parents; We grow up receiving love and seeking love, and loving others. All our life is realized in love. And as we have just seen, love is delivery. What an immense beauty! That someone can find that person with whom God calls them to share everything, body and soul, anxieties and sorrows, hopes and joys, health and disease, poverty and wealth ... The companion of Perfect path for me, that goes with me hand in hand along the path of life towards the homeland of heaven: «How beautiful, the marriage of two Christians, two united becoming one, in hope, in their desires, in their way of life, in the religion they practice! They are in a way like brother and sister, both servants of the same Lord. Nothing divides them, neither in the flesh nor in the Spirit. They are, in reality, two in one flesh; and where there is only one flesh, there is only one spirit. They pray together, they worship together, they fast together, they teach each other, they encourage each other, they strengthen each other. Side by side they face difficulties and persecutions, share their consolations. They have no secrets for each other, never shy away from each other's company; one never brings regret to the heart of the other. Psalms and hymns are sung to each other. Hearing and seeing this, Christ rejoices. To these people He gives his peace. Where there are two together, He is also present amongst them, and where He is present, evil is not (Tertullian)».

This giving ourselves totally to the other person is made complete by the commitment of marriage. Many are afraid of commitment because it ties. However, there is nothing wrong with tying yourself up to your loved one. Because tying in commitment does not mean losing freedom, but sharing it; It means to accept that I am not going to build my life alone, it means tying myself to the hand of someone I love, the hand I will pull when I run out of strength, someone who will bring me up when I need it. I tie myself to my partner for an indestructible bond, that no power in this world can break. Commitment makes me give myself totally, without conditions, without limits. It is the leap of faith made by those who believe that love can become more and more beautiful, even more compete, those who discover that there is a promise of full happiness in real love that goes beyond this world.

Marriage is not the death of love, as many think; it is the total union, body and soul, of two people who have decided to give themselves an unconditional yes, forever, capable of overcoming all difficulties; of two people who choose to bind together freely to be able to build something bigger than what each other could possibly build alone, on their own; the love of a family, the victory over loneliness.

And if love is surrender and commitment, that is why it sometimes takes the form of sacrifice. Our world invites us to never give in, not to give our arm to twist. The word "sacrifice" sounds bad to us, because we avoid suffering, and we also don't want to miss any options. However, life is made of choices. And an election always entails giving up something else. With an example you will easily picture it: if I choose to be here typing on the computer, I give up hooking up with a friend for a beer; if I choose a woman, I give up all the other women; If I choose not to commit to any, I am giving up the possibility of being with the one... See? Choice and giving something else up are two sides of the same coin: freedom.

That renunciation is sometimes a sacrifice that I have to make, to deny myself, so that the other lives and grows, or for us to be able to build something bigger together. Love is often made of small gestures, such as when a parent gets up at three in the morning because her baby is crying. They obviously don't feel like getting up and feel tired, but love makes them beat that laziness and take care of their baby; That is what your mother has done for you, probably many nights. Sometimes, in a marriage the husband has to give in, and sometimes the wife will; or sometimes both have to sacrifice for a child. These are the consequences of love. But they are not terrible, nor something to avoid. They are the inevitable consequence of living our life deeply, getting involved in the deepest of existence, letting ourselves be carried away by the desire of our hearts.

We have not been wrongly designed, our desire is good, although sometimes our desires play tricks on us and we do not do things in the best possible way. In the sexual field this could have happened to you, if you have lost your virginity and then you have decided you'd like to live it again. Do not lose sight of the beauty of real love that God calls you!

Dig up the desire from the bottom of your heart!!

May the mistakes of your past not let you lose perspective of the future that God has thought for you: a total surrender in love. Remember that once a boy had an inner image of himself. It looked like a dark, dirty, muddy stone. But suddenly, the mud opened, and from that stone came a huge nugget of gold, bright and precious. And he realized what God wanted to say: "All the evil you have done in your life has not been able to tarnish the beauty that I put in you." That's what I say to you: your heart is of gold, of pure gold, and the desire in it remains intact, even though you may have lost your virginity. Do not forget!

That desire is your compass, which guides you towards the delivery of your life in love. And through this book, God is going to restore your virginity, cleaning that mud that perhaps has covered your heart so that the gold nugget in it sprouts and you can get excited with God's project for you: surrender your whole life to love. Go for it!

Day 3

The power of faith

In order to understand how the miracle of restoring your virginity may happen in your life, you must first understand what God´s power may do in your life. And for that, faith is needed. Faith is the greatest power that the Lord has ignited in our hearts. By faith we believe that God exists, that he has created us, that he was incarnated, that he died and resurrected for us, that he gave us the gift of his Spirit, that he loves us, and that he has received full power in Heaven and on earth. This is what He Himself says: «I have been given all power in heaven and on earth» (Mt 28, 18). All power! God is almighty!

The Bible often calls God, the almighty. When the angel of the Lord appeared to Mary to announce that she was going to be the Mother of God, she asked him how that could become true, she added; «"I don't know any men." The angel gave her a proof for her to believe; her cousin, Isabel, who had become pregnant being sterile and very old: "Because to there is nothing impossible"» (Lc 1, 37).

Therefore, first of all, you need to rekindle your faith. If you have faith in God, there will be nothing impossible for you either. Another example. When Jesus spoke to the apostles about the renunciation of the goods of this world, they were scandalized because that seemed unattainable but «"Jesus looked at them and said:" It is impossible for men, but God can do anything"» (Mt 19, 26). Another time, he told them: «Truly I say to you that, if you had faith like a mustard seed, you would tell that mountain: "Move from there to here" and it would move. Nothing would be impossible for you"» (Mt 17, 20).

Many of Jesus' miracles are based on the faith of those who approach Him. There are even those who approach Jesus and just by touching him, without himself knowing, were healed by their faith.

There is a phrase from Jesus that has always overwhelmed me. If we believed it, we would be capable of anything: «Truly, truly, I tell you, he who believes in Me will also do the works that I do, and even greater, because I am going to the Father» (Jn 14, 12).

For the Lord to restore your virginity, the first thing you need is to put all your faith in Him. Although you feel you have little faith, remember that a mustard seed would be enough, so that you can move mountains. The Lord has power to restore your heart, and to perform a miracle in you. It will not be a visible miracle, which can be verified; it will be a miracle of the heart.

It is not about resigning yourself to what you have done, or continuing to go back to the past, as we mentioned earlier; it is a healing that God is able to work in your heart, through which He can renew your virginity and give you the power to live your entire chastity again, waiting to give yourself to the person with whom you will share the rest of your life. It is also a great transformation that God can - if you let him - carry out in your heart so that everything we have explained in the first chapter becomes true for you, even if you´ve already had sex.

Think that, in this way, on the night of your wedding you can give your husband — or your wife — the gift of your virginity, a heart and a body unique and exclusively for him — or for her; a pure and whole heart, restored by the Lord, sanctified and virginalized heart, that when you give yourself sexually makes you one flesh with the person you love.

It is necessary now that you stop for a moment and do an act of faith. Jesus asked us the following:

«Believe in God and believe also in me!» (Jn 14, 1). To help you in the formulation of this act of faith, perhaps the words Jesus addressed to a man who approached Him in great need may help you: «"If anything you can do anything, have compassion on us and help us". Jesus replied: "If I can? Everything is possible to those who believe". Then, that man shouted: "I believe, but help my unbelief!"» (Mc 9, 22 – 24).

May you also do this great act of faith, tell the Lord that you believe that He, who can do anything and everything, also has the power to restore your virginity and transform your life and your heart. God loves you with all his heart, he has died for you, so that you may have life, to totally renew your whole being. Tell him you believe in Him!

Do not go ahead without doing this step well, because if you do not choose to believe that the Lord is capable of doing miracles in your life, it will not happen.

We usually ask others to show us that they can do something before believing that they have that capacity; but with God it happens the other way around: «Everything you ask for in prayer, believe that He has granted it to you and you will get it» (Mc 11, 24). Believe that God can do it, and then He will.

I invite you to make a profession of faith in the power of God before continuing. You can do it with your own words. If you don't know how to do it, pray the following from the heart:

«Lord Jesus, I believe that You are the Lord and that you have all the power in heaven and on earth. I trust you, Lord Jesus, and despite my weakness and my mistakes, I put myself in your presence and say to you: "Jesus, I trust you". You know my faith is like a mustard seed, poor and hesitant; but You have told me that, although I have little faith, nothing is impossible for me if I put it into play. And for that, I put all my faith in you. I firmly believe, Lord, that you have the power to work miracles in my life and restore my heart and my virginity. I think you can clean the mud from my heart and make the gold that You put inside me sprout. I believe that You are the Lord of my life and of my heart, of my past, my present and my future, and I know that You have created me for a love that is whole. Help me never lose sight of the ideal for which your love has created me, give me your grace, so that my virginity is restored and I can fully live the path of love that you have planned for me. I believe in you, Lord».

If you want, keep saying what sprouts from your heart, from the bottom of your heart. If you do this act of faith with all your strength, you will be closer to the miracle of the restoration of your virginity.

Day 4

The importance of repentance

There is still a very important step to continue. If you have already put your faith in God and believe that nothing is impossible for Him; If you have decided to live chastity and fight for it, and you have the desire that the Lord restores your virginity, you need to deeply regret having lost your virginity.

Maybe, you lost it without being fully aware of it, or at a time when you were not clear about that subject, or when you did not believe in God or wanted to live chastity, and therefore, you did not live that event as a bad or especially serious act. All that does not matter now. The light of faith and reason now makes you understand that this was not according to the will of God, that it was not a step towards your own happiness or your fullness. It might have seemed so at the time, but that doesn't matter: the only thing that matters now is Now. From your faith in God, you can see that your sin hurt the Lord. Yes! Even if you did it without being fully aware, it hurt. And why did it hurt? For two reasons: the first, because it went against your own happiness, against your own integrity, against your own fullness. The second, because with your sin you also made another person fall, and you acted against that person´s happiness, their integrity and their fullness. It hurt the Lord because you hurt yourself and because you hurt another person.

I do not write this to arouse in you a feeling of guilt, but so that, being aware of the truth of your actions, you can repent from the heart. If you look the other way, there is no true regret. The evil we do affects the heart of God, it hurts.

God suffers from our infidelities and wants to forgive our faults, but it is necessary that, if we did turn away, we return first to Him. Thus says the prophet Osea, about the complaint of God: «When Israel was young I loved it and from Egypt I called my son. The more I called them, the further way they moved from me... (Os 11, 1 – 2)». Also through Jeremiah the Lord calls us to acknowledge our sin, repent and return to Him: «Come back, unfaithful children, I will not pout you, because I am compassionate, I do not hold a grudge forever. But acknowledge your guilt, since you have rebelled against the Lord, your God. Come back, unfaithful children: I will heal your infidelity (Jr 3, 12 – 13. 22)».

So, acknowledge your guilt; acknowledge that it hurt the Lord and it hurt you and another. Even if you don't see it clearly, trust God's word, and repent; ask the Lord for forgiveness, and ask him to restore your heart, that heal your wounds, and let the consequences of that sin be carried away. Ask forgiveness also for sinning against another person, ask Him to restore their heart also, heal their wounds and also take the consequences of that sin on the other person. It can help you to pray Psalm 50:

«Mercy, my God, for your goodness,

by your immense compassion

erase my guilt;

Wash all my crime,

clean my sin.

Well, I recognize my fault,

I always keep in mind my sin:

against you, you only, I have sinned,

and done what is evil in your sight.

So that you may be justified

in your words

and blameless in your judgement.

Behold, I was born in guilt

In sin my mother conceived me.

You like a sincere heart,

and you instill wisdom inside me.

Spray me with the hyssop: I'll be clean;

wash me: I'll be whiter than snow.

Make me hear joy and joy,

May the broken bones rejoice.

Remove your sight from my sin,

erase all guilt in me.

Oh God, create in me a pure heart,

renew me inside with a firm spirit;

cast me not away from your presence

don't take away your holy spirit

from me.

Give me back the joy of your salvation,

strengthen me with a generous spirit:

I will teach the wicked your ways,

sinners will return to you.

Free me from the blood,

oh God, God, my Savior,

And my tongue will sing your justice.

Lord, you will open my lips,

And my mouth will proclaim

your praise.

The sacrifices do not satisfy you:

If I offered you a holocaust,

you wouldn't want it.

My sacrifice is a broken spirit;

A broken and humiliated heart,

Oh God, you will not despise.

Lord, for your goodness, favor Zion,

rebuild the walls of Jerusalem:

then you will delight in right sacrifices,

offerings and burnt offerings,

steers will be immolated on your altar».

If you have already confessed that sin or those sins you committed, it is enough that you repent again and ask the Lord for forgiveness with all might, with the true desire that the Lord restores your heart. If you have not yet confessed, this is the time to do it. As Pope said: «I can and must strongly affirm that there is no sin that the mercy of God cannot reach and destroy, where he finds a repentant heart that asks to be reconciled with the Father» (Misericordia et Misera, 22).

It is not a victim like or false pain, but a pain of the heart that springs from love and trust in God. «Because I love you, Lord, I trust you. Because I trust you, I know that sin hurts you and that it has not contributed to my good. Because I know it hurt, I apologize». And so, through sincere repentance and the sacrament of confession, the Lord forgives us.

But there is a very important step to repentance, which often times we do not consider: to forgive ourselves. Only if we put ourselves under the merciful gaze of God, does He give us strength not punishing ourselves about own sins. It is about looking at ourselves with serenity, recognizing that we have misused our freedom and regretting it, striving from now on to do things right.

There are many things that could´ve lead you to lose your virginity: the passion of adolescence, the education you received, the other person who led you to do it, social or friends' pressure, curiosity, the wounds caused by another person , not being clear about the reasons for living chastity or thinking that it was not a consequence of your faith... Recognize those things, recognize how they conditioned the way you acted, acknowledge that you freely chose to do what you did, and forgive yourself. Often times, we are the toughest judges for ourselves. In order to embrace virginity in the present, it is essential that you reconcile with your past. Look at yourself as God looks at you, with compassion, and He will make you able to forgive yourself.

The last necessary step for repentance and reconciliation is to forgive the person or people with whom one has had sexual relations. Sometimes we are stuck with thorns of resentment towards the people we have loved or who have loved us. And if we have maintained relations with them, those wounds become much deeper, because we have become one flesh. Therefore, ask the Lord to give you a look of mercy on them. That does not mean that you apologize for their mistakes, nor that you keep throwing them in your face; just forgive. You may find it very difficult, it make take you a big effort.

If so, do not force yourself; do it little by little.

I remember a boy who was quite in love with a girl, and they had sex; then she left him, and they continued being friends. He told his best friend everything he felt towards her, and that it took him a lot of effort to overcome the situation... he ended up discovering that his best friend was having sex with the girl, and that they were both hiding it from him. He felt cheated, betrayed, and deeply hurt, full of anger and resentment. That resentment led him to lose himself in a spiral of alcohol, drugs and girls; all that together brought out the worst of him. And yet, that only served to increase his pain and anger. But God had a plan for him ... In an impact spiritual retreat, he had a very strong encounter with God's love. He felt a very deep love; He felt that God forgave all his sins, and gave him a new life. At the same time, God made him realize that he was bound by ropes that would not let him be free. He made him see that, in order to fully live his new life, he had to be able to forgive. And so he did. God gave him the grace of a merciful love, which led him to reconcile with his friend, and he felt relief like he had never felt before. He felt free and at peace, full of God's love.

He finally felt able to embrace the new life that the Lord had given him, leaving behind the chains with which the resentment had kept him tied.

Sometimes it takes a long time to fully forgive someone. Ask the Lord for the grace to forgive, ask him to make you able to forgive. Don't get hooked on past mistakes. Drop ballasts, so you can move on. Leave your past completely immersed in the mercy of God. If you want, I propose a prayer so you can prepare your heart for that forgiveness, and ask God to help you forgive, because without his grace it might be very difficult:

«Father of goodness, I thank you, because you have given me life and filled me with your gifts, because you have created me free and able to choose my own path. You have called me in many ways, but sometimes I have become like the prodigal son and I have turned away from you, in other ways, wasting the gifts that You had given me. I apologize, Father.

My virginity was a gift you gave me for me to share with the person you put in my path, to get to you walking side by side. I have lost it ahead of time. Now I am aware of what that means, and I am deeply sorry. Forgive me, Father. I throw myself into your arms and collapse in them with the confidence of a child, because I know that you love me, beyond what I have done, and that you welcome me again in a hug of mercy. Father, you know that it is hard for me to forgive who has hurt me.

Help me to forgive others as You forgive me. Remove from my heart the poison of resentment, and fill it with your love and mercy, so that I can share them with those who have hurt me. Give me the grace to forgive as You forgive me. Set me free from my past, break the chains of hate, so that I can fully surrender to the plan of love that You have thought for me. Thanks, Dad».

If you want, you can continue praying, with the words that sprout from your heart...

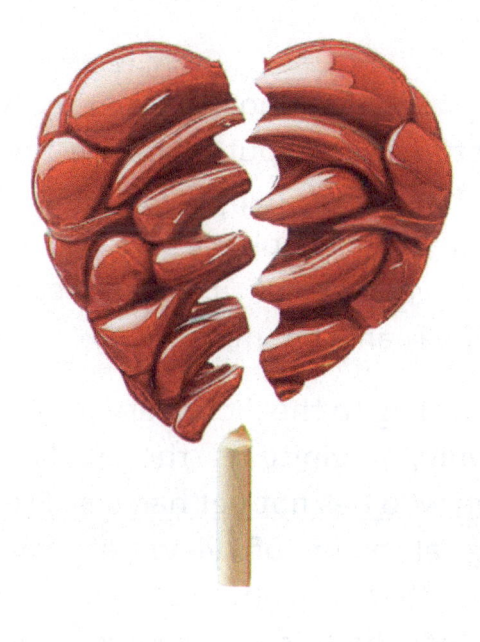

Day 5

Recover virginity

We already know that recovering virginity is not about changing the past. What happened, happened for real; and later on in this book we will also learn to take advantage of it. But recovering virginity is another matter.

According to the dictionary of the Royal Academy, virginity is the quality of a person who has not yet had sex. From the biological point of view, especially in women, there is a physical sign that is lost when you have sex. However, this sign can also be lost for other reasons. And the fact that virginity does not have a physical sign in men, that doesn't mean that men don't lose it. Therefore, we part from the fact that virginity is something that goes beyond the physical. Saint Augustine, when he writes his book The

City of God, faces the problem of the Christian virgins who were raped when Alaric sacked Rome. Did those virgins lose their virginity when they were raped? Saint Augustine strongly says no, because chastity is a virtue of the spirit; and from the spirit, the body is sanctified.

Let's look at it with an example. Jesus says the following in the Gospel: «You have heard that it was said: You shall not commit adultery. But I tell you: anyone who being married looks at another woman lustfully has already committed adultery with her in his heart (Mt 5, 27 – 28)». This text is essential to understand what I am trying to explain; If a man who is a virgin, looks at a woman and desires her sexually, Jesus says that he has already sinned with her in his heart. In that sense, that man has already lost the virginity of the heart, although he retains the virginity of the body.

Thus, virginity is a virtue much deeper than a mere physical fact, and it has to do with the heart. In fact, the great renewal that Jesus brought to the Jewish religion was to turn it into a religion that should be lived from the heart and not merely based on external signs. Because the body is sanctified from within, from the heart.

The Pharisees thought that purity depended on external acts, and Jesus fought vigorously against it, teaching that the important thing was what flowed from the heart: «Nothing that enters the body from outside can make men unclean, because it does not enter the heart. It goes into the belly and it is thrown into the latrine. What comes from within a man, what´s in the heart is that is what makes men impure. Because from within, from inner thoughts, come out the perverse thoughts, fornications, robberies, homicides, adulteries, greed, malice, fraud, debauchery, envy, defamation, pride, frivolity. All that evil comes from within and make man impure» (Mc 7, 18 – 23).

Purity comes from the heart affecting the body, and not vice versa. What Jesus is telling us here is that not only having sex I lose my virginity, but when I allow impure thoughts flow, my body also then falls into impurity and I lose the virginity of the heart. But precisely because of that, it also works the other way round. If after my heart has fallen, it burns now in chaste love and purity, will not this purity also affect my body? If having lost my virginity, I restore in my heart the virtue and desire of chastity, will this not affect the purity of my body and its virginity?

In that line are some words of Jesus, also addressed to the Pharisees: «Woe to you, teachers of the law and Pharisees, you hypocrites, who clean the outside of the cup and the plate, while inside you are full of greed and self-indulgence! Blind Pharisee! first clean the inside of the cup and then the outside will also be clean (Mt 23, 25 – 26)». That means that if you clean your heart, your body will also be clean. If the Lord, with his grace, plucks impurities from your heart, your body will be sanctified by chastity. If the fire of chastity and the light of virginity are lit in your heart, it will also shine in your body.

From here we can reread the text we have cited above in reverse. If the sins that make men impure come out of the heart, the virtues that make him pure also come out of the heart. Just as if a man looks at a woman and desires her, he has already sinned with her, if a man looks at that same woman with a pure look, purity can sprout from his heart and flood his body, making him pure. If "what comes out from within men, makes them impure," it can also make them pure.

Thus, virginity is not so much a matter of the body as it is of the heart. The Lord can give you a virgin heart, and from there he can restore your virginity.

As we are a unity (because we cannot divide ourselves, and Christianity is not a dualistic religion) what happens in our body affects our heart, and vice versa.

There is nothing more beautiful than a pure look. And a pure look can come from a person who has committed the most horrendous sexual sins, if his heart has been restored by Christ and the grace of chastity has nested in him. Nothing more sublime than a man, who is sorry to have lost his virginity, loves a woman with chastity and is able to look at her with purity and wait, to love her the way God wanted it.

But what exactly do we mean when we say heart? The Bible tells us that the heart is the seat from which a man governs his life, where feelings, desires and decisions arise. It does not refer, of course, to the physical organ, but to what we might call the center of the soul, consciousness — in fact, the apostle Saint John uses the word "heart" to refer to consciousness: «My children, Let us not love in word or mouth, but with works and according to the truth. In this we will know that we belong to truth, and we will reassure our heart before Him, in case our hearts condemn us, for God is greater than our heart and knows everything. Dear ones, if the heart does not condemn us, we may feel full confidence before God» (1 Jn 3, 18-21).

The heart is the holiest redoubt we have, the center of our soul, where everything takes place. That's where the biggest battles are fought and the big decisions are made; that is where the Lord dwells, secretly, through his Holy Spirit; and from there it is where He sanctifies our whole being, body and soul.

The virtue of virginity, although directly related to the body, has to do primarily with the heart. And regardless of what we have done and the sins we have committed, the Lord can restore virginity in our hearts, can give us a virgin heart. How? If we do an act of faith in the power of God, we repent of our sins and decide to live with a virgin heart. This is how the Lord can restore virginity in our hearts. And with the help of his grace, we can commit ourselves to live the integrity of purity in our body and in our soul, to devote our sexual capacities to the end for which He has created them: so that we may surrender ourselves with an undivided heart to the person that He will put in our way.

Notice how beautiful the expression "with an undivided heart" is. When someone consecrates themselves in celibacy to God, they are said to serve him "with an undivided heart." In the same way, when someone leaves their life of sin behind and let the grace of the Lord restore virginity within themselves, they also dedicate themselves with an undivided heart to the person with whom they will share the rest of their life.

When you've had sex with one or several people, it is as if your heart, which is made to be for only one person, has been broken and divided, surrendering to one person or people who did not love you back. In this way, the unity of the heart is lost. Well, the grace of the restoration of virginity once again unites the heart, to rebuild its unity, so that it can be given totally, in one piece, to that person for whom it is destined (in fact, the Latin word 'purus', in addition to 'pure', also means 'simple', that is, whole, in one piece).

Virgin integrity is that ability to be united within yourself, unifying all the forces of the body, soul, mind and heart, to deliver them totally to God's plan, in one's own vocation. In the case of those who are called to marriage, the chastity of courtship and marriage is focused on this unification of all forces, to put them at the service of the wife or husband, the family, and the children. Chastity in courtship allows them both to express affection according to the relationship they live, but reserving total surrender to when the commitment is final. An chastity in a marriage allows the spouses to love each other with purity, in an exclusive way, making of each sexual act an act of surrender and love that further seals their commitment, unifying all the forces of the person to surrender to the construction of the family in love.

LET´S RECAP...

When you started reading this book you began a path that will allow you to recover your virginity.

It is not going to help you change the past, but to do something greater: Allow God to completely transform your heart and restore it completely, so that you can live the dream that He has for you from all eternity.

From now on, the strongest, the greatest, begins: the itinerary that God offers you to recover what you have lost, to have a new heart. I invite you to end this chapter with a prayer in which you ask the Lord that this miracle begins to work in you. And here it is:

«Lord Jesus, send your Spirit to my heart, which is broken and divided; clean it and renew it, take it and restore it. You know which makes it dirty, and you know that there are many things that I regret and that have affected the deepest part of my heart. I want to recover my integrity, Lord, I want to recover my virginity, so that I can surrender without fissures, with a new heart; to be able to give all my life in love. Gather my divided heart and restore it, Jesus, renew it by the strength of your Holy Spirit, and fill it with your love and your peace. I beg you, Jesus, knowing that you love me, and that you always listen to me. I firmly believe that You can do anything».

If you want, you can continue praying, with the words that sprout from your heart...

Day 6

The living water of the Spirit

I often have heard in confession girls and boys who have fallen in a sexual sin, or masturbation, or had sex of any kind; and they come shattered, feeling unable to either leave that vice behind, or not fall into it again. And I always tell them the same thing. I put the example that in sexuality, we feel as if a drop of black ink fell into a large tub filled with crystal clear water. That drop of ink is spreading and blackening the water, and there seems there´s no way to separate the clean water from the murky water ... Sexuality touches our intimacy so deeply, that we have the impression that it permeates everything. It seems as if once one has fallen into sexual sins, it´d be impossible that one could become completely clean again.

Therefore, will we say that sin is stronger than grace? Or that sin can definitely sully a soul, and grace cannot definitively restore it? Can we say that if a man lusts for a woman he has already sinned with her, but not the opposite? No way! Sometimes Christians have this pessimistic mentality. To those who think like that, I´d say:

"If you haven't told a single lie for a whole month, and you lie once, are you invalidating all the times you've told the truth?".

- The answer is "No"..

- If you always obey your parents and do your homework, but one day you disobey, do you invalidate all the times you have obeyed or done your duty?".

- The answer is still no.

- Then, if you have been living in chastity for a whole month, why does a sin make you think that all the previous purity has become dirty and invalidated?

It is true that sexuality affects the most intimate part of our heart, but that does not mean that it absolutely stains our whole being, like that drop of ink that falls into the water. Due to that pessimistic mentality, and also due to sexuality touching us deep in our inner being and our conscience, we may not understand the grace that the Holy Spirit works in us; the grace of regeneration, renewal and justification.

If we talk about a drop of black ink that falls into the water, let's talk about water! Pure, crystalline water, virgin water. Water is a beautiful sign of chastity. Is there any water that simply can´t be contaminated by that drop of ink that sin represents?

In a conversation that once Jesus held at the edge of a well with a woman who´d had five husbands, and now lived with a man who was not her husband, Jesus said to her: «If you knew the gift of God and who it is who says to you "give Me a drink", you would be the one asking him, and he would give you living water (Jn 4, 10)» (Water in a well is stagnant, it does not move. Living water flows, flows and heals). The woman does not understand Jesus, and asks what water he refers to. Jesus responds: «Anyone who drinks this water will be thirsty again; but whoever drinks of the water that I will give them, they will never thirst: but the water that I give them will become in them a well of water springing up to eternal life» (Jn 4, 13 – 14).

It is evident that Jesus is talking about another water, a living water, that quenches thirst and gives eternal life. What does Jesus mean? He answers us in another passage of the same gospel: «On the last day, the most solemn of the feast, Jesus stood and cried out: "If anyone thirsts, let him come to me, and drink, he who believes in me; as the Scripture says: out of their hearts will flow rivers of living water". He said this referring to the Spirit, which those who believed in Him were to receive» (Jn 7, 37 – 39).

The Holy Spirit is the living water of which Jesus speaks! That water that quenches thirst, that jumps to eternal life. Not only cannot it cannot be contaminated, but also it cleanses and turns pure everything it touches.

Our heart, when it is hurt by sin and loses its purity, its like dead, there is no life in it. But the water of the Spirit heals it. The Holy Spirit is able to heal our hearts and bring them alive; It is able to restore purity and virginity; He is able to eliminate all the strength of sin and renew it completely.

That is what Jesus meant when he said that the water He brings becomes a spout of living water that gives eternal life and quenches thirst. And Jesus also says that this water dispenser is inside us, that we don't have to go looking for it anywhere. So, the source that is capable of regenerating our virginity is within us, in our own heart, fully accessible. How is that possible?

Jesus was baptized in the water of the Jordan River, and there he inaugurated for us the sacrament of baptism, which is the sacrament of the living water of the Spirit. Through it we received the gift of the Holy Spirit, who comes to dwell in our hearts and stays with us forever. Sometimes, the presence of the Spirit in us is lethargic, as a source that only drips down a pipe, instead of letting out all the force of the water inside. We too have all the presence of the Spirit, but not always the fruits of his grace are visible and real in us. In order for the Holy Spirit to heal our hearts and restore virginity, we must put our faith in God and believe that He is almighty and can perform miracles in us; and by confession we have to unclog the pipe, removing everything that obstructs and prevents it from flowing in all its might.

Even though we have received in baptism the gift of the Spirit, the grace of the Spirit gradually develops through our life, counting on our faith and our freedom.

When we let impurity flood our hearts, we break it´s unity and integrity. We know that the Lord can restore our hearts, and restore virginity through the grace of the Holy Spirit that we received at baptism. We can access that grace at any time, because he is always with us. Therefore, it is only necessary that we enter into our inner selves and ask the Holy Spirit to act with all his might and restore our virginity.

The work that the Spirit carries out in us is threefold: it is a work of regeneration, renewal and justification.

And what does all this have to do with recovering virginity?

St. Paul speaks to us in this way about the triple action of the Spirit in us: «Before, we too, with our foolishness and obstinacy, walked along the wrong path; we were slaves of desires and pleasures of all kinds, we spent our lives doing evil and green with envy, we were unbearable and we hated each other. But when the goodness of God our Savior and his love for mankind was manifested, not by the works of justice that we had done, but, according to his own mercy, he saved us by the bath of regeneration and renewal of the Holy Spirit, who poured out copiously upon us through Jesus Christ our Savior, so that, justified by his grace, we will be, in hope, heirs of eternal life (Tit 3, 3 – 7)».

What St. Paul wanted to tell us, in summary, is that, even after sinning, the baptism bath spills upon us the Holy Spirit to give us hope. The Holy Spirit, with his power and our faith, is able to restore what we had lost! That is why I invite you to finish this chapter by praying to the

Holy Spirit, asking for the renewal of your inner self:

«Holy Spirit, You are the living water that can quench the thirst of my heart, which can quench the flame of my vices. I apologize, because many times I have ignored your presence in my heart, and I have not been guided by you. I have followed the voice of my instincts, of the world, of bad counselors ... and I have not let you guide me. Enlighten me, Holy Spirit, come back to my heart, guide my steps from this moment so that I always choose the path of my own happiness».

Here´s a prayer form father Kentenich to the Holy Spirit which could be of great help:

«Holy Spirit, you are the soul of my soul. I adore you humbly. Enlighten me, strengthen me, guide me, comfort me.

And as far as it corresponds to the plan of the eternal Father God, reveal to me your desires. Let me know what Eternal

Love desires from me. Let me know what I should do,

let me know what I should suffer, let me know what, silent, modestly and in prayer, I must accept, load and bear. Yes, Holy Spirit, let me know your will and the will of the Father.

Since all my life does not want to be anything other than a continuous and perpetual Yes to the wishes and will of the eternal Father God. Amen».

Day 7

Regenerated by the Holy Spirit

The word "regeneration" is a strong word. The Greek word for it can literally be translated as "rebirth, regeneration, recreation, being born again." Something that regenerates is something that is completely restored. There are animals that are able to regenerate when a part of their body is amputated; some are even able to reproduce by excision.

Jesus already told Nicodemus that having faith in Him means being born again. That new birth, which is received through the Holy Spirit, is a true regeneration. Our whole being is regenerated, rebuilt and recreated. The breakdown that occurs within us is completely restored. The wounds in our heart are completely healed. This is not to be understood symbolically: the fact that something happens in an invisible way does not mean that it isn´t real.

Next to the idea of regeneration is that of restoration. According to the Royal Spanish Academy, restoring is "Recover and recuperate. Repair, renovate or put something back in the state or value it used to have".

The Lord also has restorative power, which makes us recover and get back the lost grace; His Spirit restores our heart and our virginity. Thus, the heart can return to the state it had before we lost it.

Baptism is not lost, and its fruits can be renewed every time, because it is a sacrament that prints character.

The Holy Spirit is always in us, and from within us it can regenerate us if we ask it with faith.

You can ask the Holy Spirit to heal and unify your heart, to restore your integrity and your virginity, to grant you to be "born again".

Renovated by the Holy Spirit

The Greek word "renewal" is also an expression with a very deep meaning It doesn't mean remodeling something or giving it a touch of novelty, it means "to make something totally new". According to Saint Paul, the Holy Spirit can make us truly new: «Whoever is in Christ is a new creature. The old has passed, the new has begun (2 Cor 5, 17)».. The grace of the Holy Spirit can renew us completely and make us new creatures, so that the full force of sin is left behind in our lives. Jesus himself says in the Apocalypse: «Behold, I make all things new (Ap 21, 5)».

Just as God can make us again, the Holy Spirit can give us a new heart. The prophet Ezekiel uses words that we can apply to the renewal of virginity in our hearts: «I will pour on you pure water that will purify you: from all your filthiness and idolatry I will purify you; and I will give you a new heart, and I will infuse you with a new spirit; I will pluck the heart of stone from your flesh, and give you a heart of flesh. I will infuse you with my Spirit, and I will make you walk according to my precepts, and that you keep and fulfill my mandates» (Ez 36, 25 – 27).

The pure water of baptism infused you with the Spirit of the Lord, who came to dwell in your heart. And although by sin you have lost your virginity, the presence of the Holy Spirit continues to dwell in your heart, because the gifts of the Lord are irrevocable.

From there, the Spirit can do a work of renewal in you, and give you a new spirit and a new heart; not a heart broken and disfigured by sin, but a truly new heart.

Remember what we were saying on the second day: it doesn't matter what led you to lose your virginity, or how many times you had sexual relations with people with whom you did not have the final commitment. Here and now the Holy Spirit can give you a new, brand new heart, so that you give it to the man or woman of your life, a virgin heart, completely regenerated and renewed, capable of loving with all its strength and giving yourself totally.

Saint Paul also tells us about this new life that the Spirit has come to bring us: «Take off the old man and his former way of life, corrupted by his seductive desires; Renew yourselves in mind and spirit and put on the new human condition created in the image of God: true justice and holiness (Ef 4, 22 – 24)».. Only the Holy Spirit can work the renewal of our mind and our spirit, giving us a new human condition, renewed and refunded, thus recovering the image of God and the purity of our heart.

Like Clay in the hands of the Potter

There is a beautiful image that the Bible uses to talk about God's work in us, saying that He works our mud like a potter Isaiah predicted.

Psalm 33 speaks of how God models each heart:

«He modeled every heart, and understands all his actions (Sal 33, 15)». What a beautiful thing! He modeled your heart, and he knows that the mistakes you have made, were due to your search for happiness; sometimes in a clumsy and selfish way, sometimes in a beautiful and selfless way; sometimes consciously, and sometimes very unconsciously. He understands all your actions, and his mercy covers you inside and out, heals you, restores you, regenerates and renews you. His hands continue to shape your mud, his hands - which are Christ and the Holy Spirit - continue to act constantly in you to make you a precious work of God.

When our clay doesn´t want to be shaped by the Potter

It is true that we often do not allow our mud to be shaped by God. We have not given faith to his word, and we have preferred to turn away from Him and sin, thus losing our innocence and giving our heart to whom we should not. What happened to us is what «How much perversion! As if the clay were the same as the Potter, so that the piece of art says to its architect: "He has not made me", and the vessel says to the potter: "This one does not understand anything"» (Is

29, 16). He tries to shape us, but we often don't let Him.

The Potter seeing a badly shaped vessel, could shape it again

This is what the Lord told prophet Jeremiah: "Go down to the potter's house, and there I will give you my message." So I went down to the potter's house, and I saw him working at the wheel. But the pot he was shaping from clay was marred in his hands; so the potter formed it into another pot, shaping it as seemed best to him. Then the word of the Lord came to me. He said, "Can I not do with you, Israel, as this potter does?" declares the Lord. "Like clay in the hand of the potter, so are you in my hand, Israel"» (Jr 18, 2 – 6).

God is not a handy man; He is an artist who does everything right

So that the Lord can renew your mud and give you a new and virginal heart, he only asks you two things: faith and obedience. That is, that you believe that He can do this work of renewal in you and that from now on you trust Him and obey Him, doing his will. Then He will make you a perfect work of his. Because God is not a handy man; He is an artist who does everything right.

How can the Lord shape us again, when we have lost virginity? Although we have lost our virginity and have not put ourselves in the hands of God, spoiling his work, the Artist is more powerful than all our sin. And he can take our mud, moisten it with the water of his Spirit and reshape it, renewing it completely. He can give us a new, virgin and chaste heart, according to his will.

You can now pray this text of Saint Irenaeus, in which he invites us to let ourselves be shaped by God. Read it by applying it to the renewal of your virginity: «Since you are the work of God, contemplate the hand of your architect, who does all things in a timely manner, and in the same way, He will act timely as far as you are concerned. Put in His hands a soft and moldable heart, and preserve the image according to which the Artist shaped you; keep moisture in you, so that you don´t harden and lose His fingerprints. Preserving your shape you will rise to perfection; For the art of God hides the mud in you. And for this reason, if you give Him what you are, that is to say your faith and obedience to Him, then you will receive from Him his art, which will make you the perfect work of God (AH IV, 39, 2)».

Justified by The Holy Spirit

In the text of St. Paul to Titus that we read in chapter 6, it reads the Holy Spirit, who regenerates us and renews us, also justifies us; that is to say that it makes us righteous, it justifies us. What does this expression mean? The Jews thought that one obtained justice by their own strength when they obeyed the Law, so that those who did not comply with the Law were not fair. When Jesus came, he transmitted to us the gift of faith; and St. Paul teaches that what makes us fair is not the fulfillment of the Law, since no one can fulfill it perfectly; What makes us fair is the gift of faith, which gives us the grace of the Holy Spirit. That is what the dictionary (RAE dictionary) includes in one of the meanings of the word 'justify': "to make someone right by giving them grace".

St. Paul uses the idea of justification in relation to the proper use of our body:

«You were washed, sanctified, justified in the name of the Lord Jesus Christ and in the Spirit of our God. The body is not for fornication, but for the Lord; and the Lord, for the body» (1 Cor 6, 11. 13). What St. Paul teaches us here is that we have been washed, sanctified and justified by the gift of the Holy Spirit; and invites all Christians not to return to previous sinful behavior, once the Lord has justified us.

With his words he reminds us that When the Holy Spirit justifies us, it does not do so as a foreign entity. It's not like when someone is guilty and we justify them; That would be an external justification, which does not touch the heart of the person. The justification that the Holy Spirit works is in relation to regeneration and renewal. The Spirit transforms us in such a way that our being totally justifies us, returning us to the original justice, making us truly holy and innocent before the Lord.

In one of his parables, Jesus sets the example of two men who went up to the temple to pray; one of them, Pharisee, only dedicated himself to thanking God because he was better than the others; while the other, humiliated, did not dare to raise his eyes to heaven when he prayed: "Lord, have mercy on me, I am a sinner." And Jesus says that the latter was justified and the other wasn´t.

The Lord, in order to make us completely righteous and innocent, all he wants is for us to be humble and recognize our sins before Him, and then He, by His Spirit, will work this righteousness on us and transform us completely, returning innocence to us.

One of the bad consequences of living sexuality outside the context for which God created it, (that is marriage), is that it makes us lose our innocence. To be able to recover it again the action of the Holy Spirit is necessary, which justifies us by heart (it is appropriate to clarify here that when I say "innocent" I do not mean "naive"; one can be innocent, and live sexuality innocently, that is, in a fair and beautiful way, without mixing domain or lust in it. How beautiful it is when you have sex without staining the innocence of the other, but looking together to express love as deeply as possible and giving yourself totally to the other, without reservations, with a pure and undivided heart!).

Just after the parable of the Pharisee and the tax collector to whom we have just referred, Jesus says:

«Let children come to me and do not hinder them, because the kingdom of God belongs to such as these. Truly, I say to you, he who does not receive the kingdom of God as a child will not enter it» (Lk 18, 16 – 17).

The Holy Spirit returns childhood to our heart and makes it innocent again, like a child´s heart, so that, although we may have made mistakes, from now on we begin again and do things as God commands. With the grace of God, it is never too late to start over.

You may pray like this:

«Holy Spirit, regenerate my heart! You are in me, in the deepest part of my soul. I have desecrated your temple, which is my body, for sin, but You may rebuild it.

Regenerate in me virginity, give me back my purity, bring me back to life, create in me a virgin heart! May virginity be born again in me from today, so that my whole being may be kept in order to keep it to the person with whom I will share my life.

Restore me, Lord, restore purity and virginity in my heart, so that I may realize your original plan for me. Oh God, restore me! Let your face shine on me and save me! Renew me, Spirit of God, make me again, model a new heart inside me as a potter models the mud».

Day 8

Restored by God's merciful love

So far we have charted a path to re-enact the virginity of the heart. We have recalled the importance of virginity, and the fact that even when we may have lost it, the power of faith and repentance can make us regain it, because the sacrament of baptism gives us the gift of the Holy Spirit that regenerates, renews and justifies us, thus giving back the virginity of the heart, and allowing our broken heart to reunite to give itself to the right person whom we want to share our lives. In this chapter I stop for a moment to talk about the most important of all: the love of God and his mercy...

1. God does not want puppets, but children

God wants us happy. In order to be happy, we need to be free, so that we can choose; indeed, if we did not have freedom, we would not differ from animals, and we could not be happy. We'd just live. God did not want puppets, but children; children like Him, intelligent and capable of loving. We have been given freedom so that we can attain happiness. And He did not leave us alone and blind in this world, but He laid his Law in the depths of our conscience, to show us the way that we must follow if we are to achieve happiness. However, our conscience is often blurred, and we tend to mistrust like the first man did: depart from God's plan to seek our own plans, turn our backs on his Law, and misuse our freedom. The Lord, as a good father, He awaits us patiently, and continues to bring messengers and circumstances to our lives that refer us to Him and returns us to His side—if only we see them, and listen to them. Because the Lord loves us, and He wants us to return to Him. But not because He needs us! - He doesn´t, need us, we are the ones in need for Him.

2. God is bent on our happiness

God loves us with all his heart, and he is more determined to obtain us happiness than we are for ourselves. He does not love us because He expects something from us, but because He is the Love; He is the eternal, incombustible Love that always burns. He has created us out of love, and he called us to share his own life, to live eternally in communion with Him.

3. The beautiful drama that runs through the history of salvation: God seeks us when we get lost

We often turn our backs on him and seek our own way. Then the Heart of God is wounded with love, and comes to seek us. This love drama runs through the whole story of salvation. It echoes in the Bible this complaint of God´s heart, who is in love with humanity, who seeks and finds nothing but contempt:

3.1. We find it in the prophet Isaiah, in an image of God longing, with his hands stretched out to those he loves:

«I have let myself be consulted by those who did not ask, I have found those who did not seek me; I´ve said, "Behold, behold, " to people who did not invoke my name. I had my hands extended all day towards a rebellious village, which is on the wrong track, after their projects» (Is 65, 1-2).

3.2. The prophet Oseas presents God's relationship with his people as a man's love for his wife, who he loves with all his heart; but the wife is unfaithful to him and becomes a prostitute. The husband waits for her, and finally welcomes her, repentantly, forgiving her for her infidelity:

«How could I abandon you or turn you in? My heart is touched, my entrails are shuddered. I will heal your infidelity; I will love you graciously. I will marry you forever, i will marry you in righteousness and in law, in mercy and tenderness, I will marry you in fidelity and you will know the Lord» (Os 11, 8; 14. 5; 2, 21 – 22).

The Lord welcomes us again! His loving gaze goes beyond our infidelity, heals it and marries us again.

3.3. In the Gospel according to Luke, the Lord shows us the Father as a shepherd concerned about the sheep that escaped, as a woman who carefully looks for a coin, as a father who waits every day for his ungrateful son to return, and when he finally sees him, he hugs him and kisses him and completely restores his dignity. This gospel is instrumental, and I would recommend that you read chapter 15 of Luke, because in it we see that when the shepherd finds the wayward sheep, when the woman finds the coin, when the son returns to the father's house, God throws a feast. If I had never lost the sheep, the coin, the son... he would´ve never had a celebration.

Let us focus on the parable of the prodigal son. It's as if it was necessary for the son to get lost in order to realize how valuable he was to his father.

The son asks the father for his share of fortune. (On the subject that interests us,

God has given us the gift of sexuality as a very special gift, and he has given us the gift of virginity as an immense gift to share with someone whom we must fully and forever join.) But the son leaves home, and the Bible says that he consumed his goods "living lost". The older brother specifies more, telling the father "He has eaten your goods with bad women". The father's assets were not for that, but the son uses them badly, thinking he'd be happy. If you have lost your virginity, you have misused God's gifts, wasting them. Maybe then you've converted, or you've realized you've done wrong, or you've started dating someone who wants to live purity and now you might have the desire to live it too. The prodigal son, after consuming his goods, was hungry and in need, and then he visited his inner self, realized how well he lived at his father's home, and set off on his way.

Perhaps that also happened to you, after realizing that you have made a mistake, reconsider and decide to return to God's original plan about your life. But maybe, like the prodigal son, you return with an attitude of defeat, of indignity, as a slave.

This may particularly apply to those, who may have lost their virginity unconsciously; or to those, who after having sex with other people, started dating a person who kept their virginity. Perhaps that has made you realize the gift you have lost, a gift that was not for that person or people you gave it to, but for "the one", who has been waiting for you. Therefore perhaps, you feel defeated, or humiliated, maybe it makes you somehow lower your head. But if you turn to the Father, you will not find in Him preaching but with a look of mercy. As the father of the parable, He hugs you, covers you with kisses, dresses you the best robe, puts a ring in your finger, sandals on your feet, and throws a party for you. For Him the most important thing is not what you have done, but that you realize that

He loves you with all his being, that he wants you to be happy. As we have seen throughout this book, his love, his grace, and his mercy are more powerful than all your sin. And He restores your dignity again, also as far as your virginity is concerned. He hugs you and covers you with kisses, showing you his immense love. He dresses you the best robe, not your old robe, but a new one, the best, as a sign of the regeneration that He works in you.

He puts a ring in your finger, as a sign of that covenant of love that he makes with you, of that renewal that works in you, because he makes you again, and marries you as a husband to his virgin wife; it is the new and eternal, definitive covenant he makes with you, by which he renews your heart. And he puts sandals on your feet, that you may no longer be a slave, but free; so that your feet no longer get stained as you walk. He restores the innocence of justification for you to walk in a new life. And he throws a party, sacrificing the priming calf. This expression is a sign of the death that Jesus has suffered for you, on the cross, to restore your heart.

3.4. St Paul, in the letter to the Ephesians, includes the sacrifice of Jesus:

«Christ loved his Church: He gave himself for it, to consecrate it, purifying it with the bath of water and the word, and to present it gloriously, without stain or wrinkle or anything like it, holy and immaculate» (Eph 5, 25 – 27).

You can apply this text to yourself. Christ has given himself up for you, to consecrate you, to purify you, and to make you glorious again; unblemished or wrinkle-free, holy and immaculate. Christ has given himself up for you, so that you may be happy even if you've made mistakes; He died for you, to renew your heart and give you back your virginity so that you can fulfill your vocation. Christ gives you the chance to give yourself to your future husband or wife with a virginal heart, regaining the gift you have lost, so that from now on you may put it at the service of love and dedication.

Surely this helps you turn to the Lord and experience his mercy even more deeply; so that you can feel within yourself how much He loves you; so that you may be grateful and humble to Him, and recover the simplicity and innocence of the heart.

3.5. On one occasion, a sinful woman entered Jesus' side, began to tearfully water her feet, dried them with her hair and anointed them with perfume. A Pharisee was shocked, but Jesus said to him, «Her many sins have been forgiven, for she has loved much; but whoever has been forgiven little, loves little» (Lk 7, 47).

See? If you realize your sins, repent, and begin to truly love, then the Lord forgives and restores you. Perhaps if you had little to be forgiven, you would not have realized how much the Lord loves you, and you would have loved Him little. God's love has become mercy when men introduced sin into this world. God's love has become love on the cross, to forgive and restore mankind.

3.6. All these texts, of immense beauty, that show God's love for us, his creatures, are not only collected in the Bible. The liturgy says: «Oh happy guilt that such Redeemer deserved!». And there is an ancient homily that can help you to see the love that Jesus feels for you:

«Behold the spit in my face, which I have put up with in order to give you back your first breath of life; contemplate the blows on my cheeks, which I have endured in order to reshape your deformed image, according to my image; see the whiplashes on my back, which I have accepted in order to relieve you of the burden of sins, which have been carried on my back» (From an ancient homily).

LET´S RECAP...

The Lord restores you, restores the virginity of your heart, and makes you a new creature.

The Lord transforms your past mistakes into an occasion for you to experience how much He loves you, so that you may learn and never turn way from Him or His plan of love.

Similarly, if you are going out with a person who has kept virginity, look at their virginity as a gift, as a miracle of mercy. Because that person is an image of God's love for you. Just as God does not judge you, but restores your dignity, your boyfriend or girlfriend will look at you with a love greater than whatever mistakes you made before you were going out with them. He loves you so much, he loves you with your story, with your sin; and his pure gaze upon you can also help restore your virginity; it is God himself who is looking at you with mercy so that you can heal your heart.

Do not look at having lost virginity it as a defeat, as if you've lost something that's not coming back. Look at it as a victory of God's mercy over your heart. You left sin behind for good, you have been regenerated and restored by Christ, and now you are able to keep your heart virginally until the right moment, before the loving and merciful gaze of "the one", who may now be accompanying you.

Day 9

Healing the consequences of my mistakes

One topic we haven't touched on so far is the consequences that your sexual intercourse with others may have had; I am not referring to the internal consequences on you, but to the external and objective consequences that may have followed, and which may need healing. I place this chapter here, after speaking of God's merciful gaze, because it is important that you look at it all with the view that the Lord has upon you so that God's mercy can also heal the consequences of your actions and transform them. Four, are the consequences that we have to address here, so that the restoration of your virginity is complete: the sin in which you brought down other people, the pregnancies and children that may have come, the use of the pill of the day after and the abortions that may have been committed.

1. The sin in which you made other people fall

Although we have already touched on this topic a bit in the chapter about "repentance", I feel that I must address it in greater detail. Obviously one does not lose virginity on their own. On one occasion a young guy said to me, 'I know why the devil likes sexual sins so much: because it takes two people sinning at once'. I found it a curious, and correct statement; as if the devil were killing two targets with one shot. It is true: sexual sin is a shared sin. When sexual relations are not in the realm of marriage, love, dedication, respect, and understanding, then I am sinning, and making another person sin with me, even if I am not fully aware; I'm giving the other something that doesn't belong to them; and I'm taking something from them that wasn't meant for me.

This may sound hard, but remember that you are already on the path of the regeneration of your own virginity. This view is not meant to bring you down, but to ask for healing also for the consequences that your mistakes may have had in others. Ask the Lord for forgiveness not only for having fallen into this sin, but for causing others to fall; Ask the Lord to also restore virginity in others with whom you´ve had sex; Ask him to heal the wounds your relationship may have caused in them.

In the Creed we say that 'we believe in the communion of the Saints'. This means that men, especially Christians, are united by spiritual bonds, and that the good we do reverberates in an invisible way to the good others do. Just as if I look hatefully at someone I can arouse evil in him, or if I steal something from someone I can stir up anger in them, or revenge, the same thing happens with goodness. The good we do also brings about good actions from others, and sanctifies them; not only because someone sees us do something right and wants to imitate. We are also invisible and spiritually 'connected' by the Spirit in the 'Communion of Saints', and the merits of some of us affect others, and the holiness of some also favors others. This is a great mystery. A German priest who wrote a booklet of verse prayers in the Dachau concentration camp, put it this way in one of them:

«I'm so intimately linked to mine that as well as them I always feel as just one being: of their holiness I live off and sustain myself, and I am gladly willing to die for them. I am so dearly and faithfully united to them, that from within, a voice always tells me: 'They affect your being and your life, they decide their affliction or increase their happiness».

¡They affect your being and your life! Although you may have broken up with that person with whom you had sex and you no longer even know anything about them, that doesn't mean that what you are going through doesn´t have an impact on their life. If the Lord restores the virginity of your heart, that grace also positively affects that person's life.

Therefore, this restoration of your virginity is not just for you. It can also cause the Lord to bring out good from this process for those people with whom you had sex. Look, then, towards them, and pray for them. Ask the Lord to heal those bonds, to restore your dignity. Look at them with mercy, with a look of forgiveness, try to bring before God all the resentment you may feel, or all the sadness that may cause you to think about them, and let the grace of the Spirit in, not only for you, but also for those people. Feel how the Holy Spirit influences these people from you onto them, and how God's merciful love enters their lives and heals them, thanks to the healing process you are doing and thanks to your prayer.

The Lord told us that true Christians love even enemies. Maybe you can see them as enemies, some of the people you've had sex with. The Lord does not mean to tell you that you shall be their best friend; He means that you try to forgive, that there´s no ill. To pray for their healing, ask the Holy Spirit to come to your life and transform it. I even encourage you to ask God for forgiveness for your sins, and for those of the other person. They may never do it, and as you had a part in them too, ask forgiveness from their side, so that there is no obstacle either to your healing or theirs. That is the greatest act of love you can do for those people. As saint Stephen said just before he got lapidated: "Lord, do not take this sin into account".

And once this is done, let them go. Do not stay hooked, in one way or another, or nostalgia or resentment. These people own their life; and their life is a personal love story between them and God. God takes care of them; leave them in their hands and continue on your way. You have an eternity ahead.

There may be things that you can't talk with somebody as off today, things that will remain unsaid between you and certain people who were important to you. When you come to eternal life, you will talk. I am sincerely convinced that once there, everything will become clear in our hearts and perfect reconciliation will take place between you and all those who have hurt us, and those who we may have hurt along the way.

2. Children

Although surely you have used contraceptive methods in your sexual relations, these do not prevent from a pregnancy hundred percent. Or maybe for some reason you had sex without using them. Anyway, maybe your relationships outside of marriage have resulted in an unexpected pregnancy, and a child. The first reaction when this happens, tends to be a bitter surprise and rejection. I have to admit that this fact keeps striking me for two reasons: the first, because you don't have to be a doctor in biology to know that sexual relations are directly related to the transmission of life. And secondly, because all life is worth it and it's precious in the eyes of God. Yes! I am sincerely convinced that, even when a pregnancy does not come out of wedlock and it comes in an unexpected way, it should be welcomed with joy. Because the fact that a new life comes as the consequence of an error, that doesn't mean that this new life is an error.

A life is always valuable and worth it. And a child is one of the greatest joys in life, even if it comes when you don't expect it. Parenthood gives a deep meaning to life, and makes people realise that we are not called to live for ourselves, but for others; It teaches us that our life is not to be kept for ourselves but to give ourselves away and that there is more joy in giving than in receiving. Therefore, if a new life has come into the world through your errors, you have been an instrument of God's creative action, which has collaborated with you, through your mistakes, to give birth to a new creature. This new creature is worthy of being loved and has been called to an eternal life. It's wonderful! We should never get used to the gift of life. It is a miracle.

However we must meditate on these things; no human being should come to this world in an unwanted or unexpected way. No matter how many means are put in place to prevent a pregnancy, it may still happen, because it is an intrinsic consequence of sexual intercourse. Therefore, every sexual act should be carried out with the awareness that it might lead to a new life. This is what the Church calls "responsible parenthood": it is a call to be responsible for our actions, as a consequence of our freedom assumed in a mature and joyful way.

In today´s world we´ve been sold the idea that there is a dissociation between sexuality and fertility, as if they were two different things. This often causes us to have unconscious sexual intercourse thinking that it will not have consequences. And yet, sexuality and fertility are two things that are closely related.

If you are the father of a son or daughter born from having sex outside of marriage, you may have to reconcile with your parenthood. If that pregnancy caused you perplexity or fear or anger, and if you rejected the child at first, that could have influenced your son or daughter, because we transmit to them in the mother´s bosom what we feel.

Every child has the right to a father and a mother. If this is your case, it is necessary that you reconcile with your parenthood and see your son or daughter as a gift from God, precious and worthy of being accepted and loved. Ask the Lord to heal in your children the consequences of the negative feelings you may have had towards them, so that your love for them is unconditional. Because he - or she - were not a mistake, even if that pregnancy was a consequence of a mistake.

I don't know what kind of relationship you have with your son or your daughter now, but it's never too late. Spiritually, by the communion of saints, the Lord can heal in them the wounds you have caused them if you repent and ask the Lord. And humanly you can now accept them, love and welcome them, and thus help them heal their wounds, assuming with freedom and joy the consequences of your actions.

You may have a pending conversation with your son or daughter, which may not be for now but for later ... Let yourself be led by the Spirit so that you can be God's instrument for the healing for your child. Make them aware of the infinite value of all human life, which deserves to be loved, which in fact is eternally loved by God. These human lives are called to live eternally in communion with Him, and with you.

3. The day - after pill

The distribution of the morning after pill is a very commonly extended practice in many places, and there are already many girls who use it after having sex, to avoid pregnancy. If you have ever taken this pill, or you made a girl take it, these paragraphs may stir you up a bit ...

One of the things that has been said about this pill is that it is contraceptive, but it is not abusive. You should know that this is not true. The morning after pill not only prevents fertilization, but also prevents the embryo from nesting in the uterus, thus causing imperceptible micro-abortions.

This means that sometimes the fertilization of an ovum may have occurred, but the pill has prevented this embryo, when it reaches the uterus, from developing normally, and has caused the body to expel it. Here we must not forget that from the first moment of conception, there is already a true human life, a child of God, unique and unrepeatable, to whom God has given such an immemorial soul.

If you have taken the morning-after pill, or your girlfriend has taken it after having sex, you may have provoked an abuse, even if it was unintentionally and unknowingly. If so, you may have had a child who has not arrived to develop and to be born, but by faith we know that this child, who has died innocently, is in the presence of God. This may be a strong statement for you, but you should not blame yourself, because at the time you took the pill you probably didn't even think about it, nor was it your intention.

We can´t possibly know if there had been fertilization or not, or when there has been a micro-abortion; In fact, these micro-abortions sometimes occur spontaneously without taking any drug. With regards to whether fertilization did take place or not, you will know only when you come to the presence of God. That is why I recommend that you read the following paragraphs, which may be worth to the extent that you may have had one of those micro-abortions. If so, you have a child in heaven, who loves you and prays for you.

Continue reading!

4. Abortion

Your case may be different from the one we just talked about, and maybe the previous paragraphs touched you... you may have also experienced a pregnancy as a result of your actions, and decided to have an abortion, or consented to it, for fear, out of shame, or in a more or less unconscious way. My intention here is not to stir your conscience. I do believe that it is very necessary that you become aware that abortion is a very serious act, whether caused by direct intervention, or caused in a barely perceptible way. And it is important that you become aware in order to experience God's forgiveness and healing of those events of your life.

Speaking of abortion, Pope says:

«I want to emphasize with all might that abortion is a serious sin, because it ends an innocent human life. With the same emphasis, however, I must affirm that there is no sin that God's mercy cannot reach and destroy, where he finds a repentant heart that asks to be reconciled with the Father» (Misericordia et Misera, 12).

There is no sin that escapes the mercy of God, there is nothing that God cannot forgive! In order for the Lord to heal the wounds that abortion has left in you, it is necessary that you become aware of its seriousness, and that you repent with all your heart. May you confess that sin, if you have not already done so, putting all your repentance and your pain before God.

Then it is very important that you also apologize to the possible son or daughter that you could have had. For this, something that can help you is to write a letter, and read it aloud before an image of the Lord or in a chapel, because that son or daughter is in the presence of God and from Him he listens to you... So you can reconcile with that son or daughter, whom you can see in heaven, whom you can hug, kiss and ask for forgiveness (This isn´t at all a fairytail). Through faith we know that when we cross the threshold of death, we will meet them again. Having done that, leave your son or daughter in God's hands, and move on, towards heaven, knowing that there you can have that pending conversation with him or her.

Children who have died before baptism are with the Lord, and from there, in communion with Him, they are holy. And for that very reason, they are able to forgive those who did not let them be born, because they love with the same love of God from heaven.

Rest assured that your son or daughter does not hold any resentment, but forgives and loves you, and that he is looking forward to heaven to be able to hug and comfort your heart themselves. And besides, since they are saints in the presence of God, they intercede for us, like all saints. So if you have a son or daughter who is already with the Lord, he or she is praying for you...

I know that these thoughts may be bittersweet, but they are true: God wants to heal this wound of your heart too, and he can, because he is almighty. You do everything on your part to reconcile yourself with God and with your son or daughter, and then just leave it to the mercy of God, and move on...

Certainly, there are lessons you should learn from it all. When someone deeply repentant has confessed to me that they terminated a pregnancy, I have invited them to become a defender of life for the rest of their days; and this invitation has always been very well received by them.

I tell you the same thing: your testimony could prevent abortions taking place. Become a staunch defender of life from the first moment of conception, and deal with your testimony so that others do not make the same mistakes you made, so that they do not have to suffer the consequences either...

LET´S RECAP...

You can be a true beacon of light in the middle of this world.

The Lord can use your mistakes and draw good from them, and He may turn you into an instrument of his healing and mercy. So, draw the teachings that the

Lord wants from this mistake you made, and thus redeem it, so that it reverts for the good of others.

Seal with the grace of God's mercy your past and ask the Holy Spirit to heal that wound, the consequence of your mistakes.

You can experience an even deeper regeneration of your purity and virginity, and you will begin to live a new life today, free from all the chains your past tied you to.

Look at yourself with the gaze of God. And from there, start over...

And from that look, I invite you to raise a prayer to God the Father, so that he heals the consequences of your mistakes, in you or in others:

«Father of Mercy, you are so Kind! Your Mercy with me knows no limits. You are able to heal the consequences of my mistakes, and even take good out of evil.

And this miracle is what I need, Father. Heal the consequences that my sin may have caused in those people with whom I´ve had sexual relations (you can remember their names and place them before God); Help them meet you and respect themselves, and heal their wounds.

(If you have children:) I thank you for....., Who were a gift from you. Although they have come to life because of my mistake, they are not a mistake, but a gift of your love that makes my life meaningful. Bless them and protect them; Heal in them the consequences of my own wounds. May they always feel surrounded by your love.

(If you've taken the morning - after pill:) Father, I put before you that moment when I took (or had my partner take) the morning after pill, refusing to assume the consequence of my actions, and perhaps causing an abortion, even without knowing it. Heal the wounds that this fact could have caused in me and in my partner. I know that, if there was a pregnancy, I have a child before you, who is interceding for me. Help me, Father, to get where he is, in your presence, so that I can reconcile with him and give him the hug I never had the opportunity to give him. (If you have aborted:) Father, I put before you the moment (or the moments) when I decided to abort (or pressured my partner to abort); Now I know that it was a mistake, and that I had no right to decide on the life of my son (s) or daughter (s). Father, heal that deep wound of my being, give me a new heart. I know that my son (s) or daughter (s) is with you, interceding for me. Help me, Father, to get where he (is), in your presence, to be able to reconcile with him (them) and give him (them) the hug that I never had occasion to give him (them).

I put all this in your presence, Father, because I fully trust in you and I know that you are Mercy itself. I need you, Lord, I need your healing power. Heal me and set me free, so that from now on I can live a new life. Amen».

Day 10

A look of wisdom on one´s own life

In this chapter I want to offer you a series of tools so that you can take a wise look at your own sin story. What is a wise look? Wisdom books are those books of the Bible that reflect on the history of the people of Israel and draw teachings that become wisdom for the whole world.

To take a wise look on your own life is to look at it wisely, in order to learn. That look must be a look of faith, allowing you to see how God carries out his plan in all things and through all circumstances. God is provident, takes care of us, and his plan of love cannot be frustrated. Everything comes together so that God's plan of love may go ahead: the circumstances of our life, our own freedom, and even our sin. Yes! our sin plays a part also.

I invite you now to take a wise look on the fact that you lost your virginity. Let's look at that fact from faith, so that the Holy Spirit will give us wisdom to draw the lessons that God would want us to learn. The foundation we are going to start from Saint Paul´s words: "And we know that in all things God works for the good of those who love him" (Romans 8:28).

God´s will is mysterious. It works in two ways: sometimes God wants something and does it; sometimes God does not want something, but allows it to happen. Why? Because God gave us freedom, and He does not take away our freedom. When he created us free, he did it so that we would choose good and, according to his will, be happy. But he knew that we could also misuse our freedom and use it to go against his will, thus making ourselves unhappy.

When God gives us a gift, He doesn´t take it away from us. He has given us freedom, and even if we misuse it, He still lets us free. This is why God allows many things to happen in our lives; because they are a consequence of our freedom or the freedom of others.

In addition, God allows us to misuse our freedom and does not prevent it because of something very important: God is the only one who has the power to bring out good from evil. It is not that God wants evil to happen, He does not want that; but he allows it because he respects our freedom, and also because he has the power to obtain good from that evil. Only He can do it. From the evil of his Son's condemnation on the cross, God drew our redemption and it was the deepest demonstration of love that He could do. Thus, God transformed a sign of torture and death into an instrument of love and reconciliation; Therefore, the cross today is not a sign of punishment for us, but of God's merciful love.

In the same way, God can bring out good from the evil you have introduced in your life, also from the fact that you have lost your virginity. The look towards that fact must not be defeatist. Often, the first reaction of someone has lost their virginity and realize that they´ve made a mistake is to feel ashamed and want to look the other way; never think about it again and try to leave it behind. Actually, acting that way signals that you have not overcome that sin, it is a sign that you have not forgiven yourself.

However, you have repented. That is why God regenerates your virginity, and makes all the forces of your heart unified, so that you can surrender to the person with whom you will share the rest of your life. With your healed heart and your recovered virginity, you can look back with a grateful and sapiential look, so that out of that harm in your life the Lord may sprout blessings.

The seven blessings that the Lord brings forth from your past

1. El The first blessing that the Lord wants to bring forth from your past is that you realize his immense love and mercy. It's all we have said in the previous chapter. God has shown you that he loves you, to the point that he gives his life for you and forgives your sin. Perhaps, had you not sinned, you would´ve never realized the immense love that God feels for you, you would´ve never experienced that his mercy is eternal. Through your fault, God has shown you how precious you are to his eyes, he has shown you that he will not allow anything or anyone to take you away from Him. Through your error, you may understand the value that the cross of Christ has for you in particular - not for all men, not in general, but for you specifically - so that you can say like Saint Paul: «Jesus Christ came into the world to save sinners, and I am

the first one» (1 Tm 1, 5); «I am crucified with Christ; I live, but it is not me who lives, it is Christ who lives in me. And my life now in the flesh, I live in the faith of the Son of God, who loved me and gave himself for me» (Gal 2, 19 – 20).

2. The second blessing that the Lord wants to bring forth from your past is that you see his power of transformation. He, with the power of his Holy Spirit, transforms your heart and restores your virginity, regenerates you, renews and justifies you. You can experience in yourself that power of God and be filled with joy, because nothing is impossible for Him; and full of joy, worship and praise will sprout in you, because you will have experienced how good the Lord is and you would´ve seen His greatness. Remember that the Lord is almighty. Not only to create the world and what is in it, but to recreate your own heart and do a wonderful work in you, filling your life

with meaning, and giving your future a new perspective. His power has renewed you so that you can surrender yourself virginally to the person you love. That's how great God is!!

3. The third blessing that God wants to bring forth from your past is humbleness. Experiencing his forgiveness and how He restores your heart and welcomes you with mercy makes you humble, aware of your poverty and your weakness, so that you realize that you need him. The recognized and forgiven sin ends our pride, our self-reliance and our vanity; it makes us poor in spirit and makes us like children; it makes us aware that if it were not for the grace of God, we would be nothing; It makes us see that it is his grace that prevents us from falling into the deepest misery... And so, it makes us humble at heart. And similarly, it helps us not to judge others, and that we do not consider ourselves better than others.

Deep down, this wisdom look on our sin can make us more holy.

4. The fourth blessing that God wants to bring forth from your past is the healing of the people with whom you´ve had sex. It's very important that you close each of the ties that may remain open in your heart with each of the people with whom you´ve had sex. It is necessary that you think about each one of them, that you try to forgive them truly, that you ask the Lord to forgive this sin and heal your heart, to undo in them the bad fruits of those relationships that you had, and to close the bond that may still keep you tied; and finally, that you put that person, his destiny and his happiness into the Lord´s hands. It is very important to make this prayer with faith, and leave that relationship or those relationships into the Lord's hands. He, with his power, will listen to that prayer, unmake those ties and, as far as possible, heal the hearts

of those people too. And after that, don't think about it anymore. Remember: leave the past to God's mercy.

5. The fifth blessing that God wants to bring forth from your past is the virtue of prudence. You know how easy it is to sin and slide down the wrong path. That should make you prudent, so that you do not put yourself on the occasion of sinning or making others sin. Prudence takes fear away, but be careful. When Jesus forgives the public sinner, he says: «I do not condemn you either. Go ahead and sin no more» (Jn 8, 11). An even stronger invitation to prudence is given when Jesus heals a paralytic, and says: «Look, you have been healed; Don't sin anymore, so that something worse may happen to you» (Jn 5, 14).

Thus, learn the lesson that the Lord has shown you through your mistakes, and be prudent. When you´ve already had sex, it is easier to reach the same point yet again with somebody else, because you have already skipped the natural barriers built by your modesty, until you give yourself away the first time. Therefore, caution is needed, as well as re-raising those barriers of modesty, so that your heart becomes virginal again, and remains.

If that happens, the Lord can restore it again, of course, because it is almighty but for your part, learn the lesson of prudence, so that once restored you do not sin anymore. Once someone loses virginity or has often times they tell themselves if I have already sinned, what does it matter that I do it again? I can´t go back, and thus get carried away ». It is the voice of the enemy that makes you believe that there is no going back, and that he wants you to let yourself be dragged so that passion and instinct become the masters of your heart. God wants you and Him to be the owners of the impulses of the heart. Learn, then, the lesson of prudence.

You may remember the parable of the prodigal son, of which we have spoken in another chapter. They say that this son was in the father's house for several years enjoying his love and reconciliation with his brother. But after that time, his past began to seduce him again. He remembered how he had fun at those parties, with that money, with those women... It had gone wrong once, but what if it was just bad luck? What if this time it went well? Why not try your luck again? Finally, he took all his goods, and one day, at dawn, before his father and brother woke up, he left again, and returned to that country where they already knew him. He came again with money, and friends returned, parties returned and women returned. He had a great time! This time it was not like the first one, he had almost forgotten the delights of that life away from his father's house... But the money ran out again, and all those people around him again left him alone.

Again, he was in need, hungry, and ended up covered in rags, begging for a crumb of bread. He thought: How can I go back to my father's house now, after all? I can´t go back. I would lose my face in shame, my father is very kind and would not reject me, but I don't feel worthy of abusing his trust again.

And my brother? If he got angry the first time, now he won't talk to me again... No, I better live like a beggar than go back home. After breaking my father's heart again, how could I look at him in the face...? While he was meditating with his head down, lying on a street in that city, suddenly someone approached him. He raised his head. It was his father, with tears in his eyes and a smile on his lips: «My son, my son! I've finally found you!».

The father pounced on him and almost threw him on the floor, hugged him and covered him with kisses. At first the boy did not know how to react, but finally hugged his father and they cried together. The father picked him up, took him to an inn and healed his wounds. He bought him new clothes and, after perfuming him, mounted him on his horse and took him back home. That day the son finally understood his father's love. He understood that Father God will always welcome us, and will keep his arms open to receive us if we move away even again and again. He knows that if we sin again, we will suffer again. But He will always remain to welcome us and heal our wounds. There the son understood that if the Father asks us to forgive the one who offends us, up to seventy times seven, it is because that is precisely what He does with us himself.

God knows you can sin again. Do not be afraid. There is never a point of return, there is no place where God's mercy cannot reach. Be prudent, realize where you have fallen, and as far as possible, be consistent, and try not to fall again. But if you do, you already know that the Father will welcome you, always, over again.

6. The sixth blessing that the Lord wants to bring forth from your past is care, in a double direction: care for yourself and care for your boyfriend or girlfriend. When you recover your virginity and the Lord restores it in your Heart, it is very important that you keep yourself for the right person and for the right time. You may now or later have a boyfriend or girlfriend with whom you want to build a future, and think: "He or she is the one." Well, remember where you've come from! And don't go back there.

In the first chapter we said that marriage is the commitment by which one chooses to surrender unconditionally and forever to another person. That commitment is sealed with the grace of the sacrament of marriage, whereby God grants spouses the gift of loving each other with the same love Christ loves his Church.

It is only after the ratified commitment to the grace of the sacrament has been sealed that the total surrender of the body and soul makes out of two people only one flesh. Wait, no matter how strong you may feel, keep yourself. You are not sure that this is the person you are going to marry until you do marry them. Don't say, "What difference does it make one day before or a day after?" A lot! Because between one day and the next an incredible miracle has taken place: God has united you with the indissoluble bond of the Holy Spirit.

From faith, we know that it is the sacrament of marriage validly celebrated that makes him or her The one. For that reason, until that moment they are not. If one who is going to be ordained a priest decides to celebrate a Mass the day before being ordained, not only does the miracle of the presence of Christ in the bread and wine not happen, but it is also a serious sin punishable by the Church88. In the same way, until man and woman have not given their will for life, sealing it with the grace of the sacrament of marriage, sexual relations between them are not a source of holiness, but sins.

7. The seventh blessing that the Lord wants to bring forth from your past is testimony. Most young Christians today are not clear about the issue of premarital chastity or want to live by it. You, with your experience, can be a witness to teach others through your testimony the importance of virginity and waiting. You can help other young people a lot so they don't make the same mistakes as you.

Since everybody is free to do what they want, even if you show them the truth, people may listen to you or may not; but at least you did your part...

Thoughts in the line of how are you going to lecture when you screw up yourself? These thoughts come from the enemy. One can be witness to the truth, even if they are not up to what they preach. I may know that something is not the right even if I sometimes fall into it; but that doesn´t make it okay. The truth is the truth, regardless of who says it.

Pope Paul VI once said something that you can apply to yourself today: «The man of today listens with more pleasure to witnesses than to teachers; and if you listen to the teachers, it is because they are witnesses». Take out the teachings of your own mistakes and share them with others, to help them keep a virtue that you may not have been able to keep. It is a love duty!

Already in the previous chapter we looked at tools to help us take a wise look at the consequences that the loss of virginity has brought, and how God can obtain good even from them, because God uses everything to carry out his love plan. Do not be afraid and return your gaze to the past with a free, reconciled and grateful heart.

LET´S RECAP...

It is important that you carry out an act of purification of your memories. Looking at those moments when you lost your virginity and had sexual intercourse can be something that moves you or ignites inappropriate desires in you.

That´s why it is important to carry out a purification of your memory, which you can do by taking a wise look on your own sins and then also God will purify with the grace of the Holy Spirit.

This will help you not to look back at those moments either from the perspective of the pleasure you had, or from the perspective of the mistake you made; but from the perspective of how that experience helps you to truly love the person you are with - or who you will be with - and to live holiness.

Thus, those memories will remain in your mind as what they are: things you did nevertheless, which do not determine your life and the Lord uses them to obtain a greater blessing for you.

I propose that you do this prayer so that the Lord can purify your emotional memory:

«Lord Jesus, You know all my history; My past, my present and my future are present before your merciful gaze. You know that sometimes my past haunts me, and my memories come to me, and they hurt me, because they make it hard for me to love myself well and love others well. Lord, purify my memories. I do not ask you to take them from me, for they are something that is part of me and where you will obtain some blessing; but I do beg you to purify them, so that they only serve me to love more and in a better way people around me, and especially, that person with whom I share or will share the rest of my life. Heal my emotional memory, so that those memories do not lift wounds, but serve me to help others. Turn my mistakes into blessings and thus You may be glorified even through my own sin. Because only You have that power. Thank you, Lord Jesus. Amen»

Day 11

Hand in hand with Mary and Joseph

Before coming to an end, I must share an open secret with you: Mary is the great gift that God has given to humanity. In her, our humanity has reached its summit, raising to God´s height. She is the finished and perfected image of what we are called to be. Humble, poor, simple, pure... all the attributes fall short. The company of Mary and her intercession are extremely powerful.

On one occasion, a youngster far from the faith told me: «I don't understand why you call Mary "The Virgin". It doesn´t sound right! I had never realized that the main characteristic by which we usually name Mary is precisely virginity. She is the Virgin par excellence. She dedicated her whole being to God and to chastity, with an undivided heart, totally devoted to God's plan. That is why it is said of Her that she is both Virgin and Wife, Virgin and Mother. Virgin, because she retains her integrity, and Wife, because she gives herself totally to the Lord her God. Virgin, because her whole being was only for God, and Mother, because she gives birth to the Son of God and to the children of the Church.

Mary knows and understands our weakness, and

«Shines on our path as a sign of consolation and of firm hope». She intercedes for us and "gives birth" to us spiritually. Therefore, She also has to be present in this regeneration that the Holy Spirit makes of your virginity, because She can also help you be born again.

How? Firstly, take Her as a model. Starting today, commit yourself to fighting to become like Her, to live purity as She lived it, to have a virgin heart at the service of God's plan for your life. Secondly, ask her to pray for you. She is the most powerful intercessor before her Son, Jesus, and as we all know, a good son never denies anything to his mother ... So take advantage of this direct call to put pressure on the Lord. Thirdly, keep her always in mind. She walks by your side; only often times you don't realize ... But she is there. She takes care of you, like a good mother who clothes her children while they sleep or throws their clothes to wash without them noticing. If you keep her in mind, you will see a multitude of gestures in which She helps you to become holy. And specifically, for our subject, if you are attentive you will see how She helps you to have a virgin heart and to live chastity.

If you are a man, ask Mary to grant you the grace of looking at your girlfriend with the same purity with which you would look at Her, and to keep her as a precious treasure, as you would do with

Her. If you are a woman, ask Mary to make you like Her, chaste and dedicated, capable of bringing out the best in others and helping men to live purity.

Remember that we are in the communion of saints; what some of us do reverts in others. This, of course, applies in a special way to the saints. So keep Mary in mind, because She is taking care of you and praying for you.

I suggest that you do this prayer that asks Mary for purity, composed by Father Jopeph Kentenich while in the Dachau concentration camp:

«Hail, Mary. For your purity, keep my body and my soul pure. Widely open your heart and the heart of your Son. Give me the grace of a deep self-knowledge, of perseverance and faithfulness to death. Entrust souls and people to me, and take everything else for you. Amen».

Also go to Saint Joseph, her husband. Let me tell you something about him that impresses me a lot. Saint Joseph was married to Mary, and surely, he expected to live into a normal marriage with Maria, if you understand me... But it turns out that Maria is pregnant and he thinks that this pregnancy comes from the relationship between her and another man, then decides to divorce her in secret. An angel appears to him and tells him to accept Mary, his wife, because that creature comes from God. Joseph, who planned to have a normal marriage, finds that he has to live with a woman who will remain a virgin throughout her whole life and with the Son of God.

Imagine how difficult! It is as if Joseph is "imposed" by chastity. He could have revealed himself, looked for life, or what not... but he remains chaste and faithful. Why? Because he knows that God's plan to save humanity is more important than his human aspirations. He knows that sexuality is at the service of love, and not vice versa, and that is why he is able to live chaste and to assume his vocation in chastity, surrendering his whole being to the service of the salvation of humankind, caring for Mary and Jesus.

How hard to understand this is! However, it´s beautiful! San José is a model of chastity for us. Ask also for his intercession, so that Mary's husband also prays for you, and the Lord regenerates virginity in your heart and grants you to put your sexuality at the service of love and giving, as he did.

Perhaps you can use this prayer to Saint Joseph:

«Blessed Saint Joseph, husband of Mary and custodian of the Lord. You lived chastity in a time similar to ours, in which purity was seen as a curse and waste; but you were faithful and in spite of the difficulties, you persevered in chastity and made it the perfect way to give yourself to your wife, your Son and God's plan. Intercede for me, so that I have a pure heart like yours; so that my gaze reflects purity, and so that, in the midst of difficulties and temptations against chastity, I know how to be faithful to my commitment to God, as you were, so that my resignation will serve to better fulfill God's plan. Amen».

Do not forget that you have a guardian angel who always accompanies you. Ask him to pray for you, and take care of you on your way. Psalm 91 says: «He has given his angels orders to keep you in your ways. They will take you in their palms, so that your foot does not stumble on the stone». Your angel can protect you, take care of you, guide you and help you not to stumble on the stone of impurity, so that your foot walks safely along the path of holiness.

I offer you a simple prayer to the guardian angel; It is very short, you can learn it by heart and pray it often, especially when you see yourself in difficult or sinful situations:

«Angel of God, who has been entrusted to me by divine providence, enlighten me, keep me, guide me and protect me. Amen».

If you want, you can put yourself under the protection of two saints who rather died than lose their virginity. I am not going to tell you about her life, but I invite you to look for them and ask for their intercession: they are Saint Mary Goretti and Saint Pelayo. Ask them to intercede for you. And I also pray for you, and I offer my life for all who read this little book, so that the Lord may work in you all the miracle of the regeneration of your virginity.

Ask for the intercession of all the saints, especially the saint of your name or the saints of your devotion. Through the communion of saints, we believe that their prayer is effective and they make our way much easier.

Day 12

Workplan

What you've read so far was aimed at helping you understand what it is to recover your virginity and how you may do it. Now I invite you to begin a personal process in order to allow the Lord to restore your virginity. This chapter will be like a fleeting summary of everything you have read only with concrete proposals, which I encourage you to follow one by one, so that you can experience in a concrete way the restoration that the Holy Spirit wants to work in your heart.

If you have not yet confessed to a priest having had sex before getting married, it is time to do so. But even if you have already done so, it might help you to put those sins back in confession before the merciful gaze of God, so that He can forgive and heal all that may have been left of it; By doing this, you will become more aware of his forgiveness and the mercy of God will enter your life in a new way. Sometimes we may confess a sin, but repentance is not total. You may confess again, after reading this book, and it might help you to definitely confess with perfect repentance. Find a priest who can understand and help you, and explain what you are going to do.

Take paper and pen, because it is important that you do not do this lightly, and writing is a way of recording what you are going to do in an alliance document between God and you, which you can then sign and even renew at some other time in your life if necessary. Find the right place: it can be an oratory, a church, a chapel ... or in your house, before a crucifix, or an image of Jesus, or Mary ... or a significant place. You may do this alone or together with someone important to you. Perhaps, if your current boyfriend or girlfriend knows about your story and knows what you are going to do, they can be a good companion and witness of this very important moment for you. It is something intimate, and it is not to be shared with many people, you may realise for yourself the best way to do it in order to help you and others.

I propose next steps so that you carry out everything you have read in this book. Do not read the conclusion of the book until you have done the following!!

1. Put yourself in the presence of God, before an image or in a chapel. Be silent in your heart, and become aware of what you are going to do.

2. Do an act of faith in God. Tell him that you believe in his power, that you believe that he can restore your virginity and regenerate your heart. Do an act of faith in what He has taught us about virginity until marriage, and tell him that although

you have not believed it or lived it, today you accept that truth and that you want to live chastity from now on. I invite you to make this sentence spontaneous, and to be able to write it, and then read it aloud, or in a low voice, whatever may help you the most. Find below a prayer that may help you write your own:

«Father of Mercy, I put myself in your presence, in the presence of your Son and the Holy Spirit. I firmly believe, Lord, that you love me with your whole being, that you have given me life and that you call me to live forever with you. I do an act of faith in your power, Lord; I confess that you are almighty and that you have the power to heal my heart and restore my virginity. Now I accept, Lord, the meaning that You have given to my sexuality, although I have not lived it well, and from now on I commit myself with you to live it according to your will».

3. Repent of your sins. If you have not confessed yet, it is time to do so. And even if you have already done so, it may help you to return to the confessionary. In any case, repent again and ask the Lord for forgiveness for sinning and for having caused others to sin, also ask forgiveness from others who have sinned with you, ask forgiveness for the consequences that your actions may have had, especially if you have committed or been able to commit an abortion. Remember that there is nothing that God's mercy cannot forgive. And also renounce the resentment that may be in your heart towards people with whom you´ve had sexual relations, for that link to be cut and stops binding you, so that you are freed. I invite you to write a prayer of forgiveness; and then I offer you a prayer that may help you write your own.

«Father of mercy, I apologize for losing my virginity too soon. (It can help you to apologize for each of the specific people with whom you have had relationships). I apologize because I also made those people sin; I ask forgiveness from you, because they may never ask you for forgiveness. Do not take these sins into account. I apologize wholeheartedly for the consequences that these sexual relationships may have, on me or others (here you can think of diseases, children or abortions). I put everything under your merciful gaze, because I know that there is nothing impossible for you and that you love me with your whole being, and I firmly believe that You forgive me all these sins».

4. Remembering everything you've read about the regeneration, renewal and justification that the Holy Spirit can work in your heart to restore your virginity, ask the Holy Spirit with faith in the name of Jesus to restore your virginity. Believe firmly in his power, and open your heart

completely, so that He can enter again and do this work in you. Do this prayer with total confidence and as passionately as you can, because through it you will place all your trust in the power of God. I invite you to write it, and then I offer you a prayer in case it helps you to write your own personal one...

«Holy Spirit, come to me in the name of Jesus! Flood my body, my soul, my mind and my heart! Completely fill my whole being! Today I ask you in the name of Jesus to work the miracle of the restoration of my virginity. Nothing is impossible to you, because You are God almighty. Regenerate my heart and restore it; renew my heart, give me a new heart, create it in me from scratch, so that from today I can love virginally again; return to my heart the innocence that I have lost. Unify all the pieces of my heart, and make it one again, make it a virgin heart, so that I can totally surrender myself only to the person with whom I will seal my love in the sacrament of marriage. Turn me into a virgin again, Holy Spirit, You can do everything! Create in me a pure heart, restore me, may my whole being be placed now and forever at the service of God's will in my life».

5. Believe firmly that this miracle has happened in your life and give thanks for it, remembering the word of Jesus that we read above: «All that you ask in prayer, believe that you have received it and it will be yours (Mk 11, 24)». So a Christian has to pray! Write a prayer of thanksgiving in which you confess that the Lord has already done this in you, and let yourself be filled by the joy of the Holy Spirit with a regenerated and renewed heart. I offer you a prayer that may help you to do yours.

«I thank you, Father, Lord of heaven and earth, because I believe and I know that You have just restored my virginity in the name of Jesus and by the power of the Holy Spirit! Thank you, Father, for your love, thank you for your regeneration, thank you for making me born again, thank you for giving me back my virginity!

Thank you, Lord Jesus, for coming to redeem me and save me, for showing me the path of Life, for giving me the chance to be born again through baptism that has now been renewed in me! Thank you, Holy Spirit, for regenerating and renewing my virginity, for making me righteous and holy again, for giving me the grace of a new opportunity! Praise and bless you, Lord, for your infinite mercy! Glory to you, Lord!»

6. Commit to keeping your virginity until marriage, and to respecting those people you may meet before marriage.

Once the Holy Spirit has restored your virginity, seal it with seven locks! Keep it with zeal, commit to guarding the purity in your heart, and to give yourself totally and only to the person you join forever in the sacrament of marriage. Write this commitment before God; I offer you a trial to help you do your own.

«Father of goodness, after this work of your love in me, I commit myself before you to keep my virginity from now on, in order to give myself only to the person with whom You join me through the sacrament of marriage. I want to live my purity and keep my heart intact; I want and I commit to strive to do things well and to guard my heart virgin until it is time to finally give myself to my husband. And I also pledge, Lord, to respect the people with whom I share my path, so that their heart will only be given to the person with whom they will share the rest of their life, be it myself or someone else. Let your will be done, Father!»

7. Ask the Lord for his help with this, and ask him to seal this restoration of your heart, because without his grace we can´t do anything. I encourage you to write it down.

«Lord Jesus, You told us that without you we can do nothing. You know how weak I am, please help me, Lord! I want to remain firm in this commitment that I just sealed before you. Give me your grace, so that I can be chaste and keep myself until it is time to surrender; and if I fall along the path, reach out to me so that I can rise again, because your mercy has no limits. Seal with your precious blood this restoration of my virginity, Lord Jesus, so that by your grace and in your name, I may transform and renew my whole life».

8. Ask the Holy Spirit for the gift of wisdom to look at your past with a wise look, so that He can bring out good from your bad actions, and enlighten you, giving you a new look towards your past. So that you may learn from it and purify memories. I offer you a trial prayer.

«Holy Spirit, you who have restored virginity in my heart, give me a look of wisdom on my past, so that I look at my life as the Father does, and with your grace, I may learn from my mistakes, so that it all may serve my good and that of others. Holy Spirit, bring out good from the bad actions of my life. Holy Spirit, enlighten me and purify my memory, so that I do not look at the past with longing or guilt, but with a look that knows how to read the providence of God in everything. I give you my past, Holy Spirit, especially my mistakes and sins. May you bring life out of it all».

9. Finish this act with a prayer to Mary, "the Virgin." She kept her whole being pure at the service of God's plan. Hand in hand with her you can recover innocence and learn to walk life like Her, loving with an undivided and chaste heart. Write a simple sentence; she is your mother.

«Mother Mary, intercede for me, so that I may live this new commitment that I have sealed today with your Son. Take me by the hand, and help me to be pure like You; Give me a heart like yours, and help me to be faithful to this commitment. Teach me to love, bring my innocence back. Protect me from all evil. Amen».

10. Once you have everything in writing, read it; or better, pray it. It can help you to read it out loud, slowly, from the heart. Do not hurry. Remember people, situations, put all the

circumstances of your past sexual life under the gaze of God. Believe firmly that the Holy Spirit is working this regeneration in you, and He will do it. Don't pretend to feel anything; Just do an act of faith. Often times, faith does not make us feel anything, but it gives us the certainty that we get what we ask for. And when you finish praying, put the date, and sign it. That date will mark the point of no return, in your virginal life. And that signature is your alliance with God, who will accompany you and help you live a new virginity.

Then, with that document, you can do several things. It may help you to offer it to the Lord in some church, sanctuary or oratory; You could also make a small bonfire (with care) so you burn it. Fire is a sign of purification, and it can also represent your desire for this commitment to reach the Lord.

It may be beautiful to be kept by your boyfriend or girlfriend, as a kind of commitment that he or she is also involved, that reminds you every time you see your new life and your renewed desire to keep yourself for him or her. Or you can save it yourself, like a treasure that gives you strength to keep on, every time you see it, as a stimulus to remain faithful to this new alliance. You may also remember or renew it whenever you need it, or whenever you are struggling again to live chastity.

In any case, it would be beautiful if you put a sign in your room that specifically reminded you of the commitment of your new virginity: a small cross, that reminds you of that redemption that Jesus has made of your sin; an image of Mary, that reminds you of that purity that She can help you to live, or some picture of your saint (or of some saint to whom you have devotion to), so that from heaven they help you in your particular struggles... Maybe you can wear a ring as a sign of that new alliance, to help you every time you see it and remind you that your life and your past have been renewed, or a cross or medal of the Virgin around the neck ... Human beings have a symbolic mentality, and signs help us remember and keep in mind what matter to us.

My advice is to look for a specific sign to help you. Put your creativity to work! Live this new life that the Lord gives you, hand in hand with Mary and with the strength of her Holy Spirit.

Remember: «If anyone is in Christ he is a new creature. The old has passed away, behold, the new has come» (2 Cor 5, 17).

We reach the end of this book. If it has served the purpose for which I wrote it, it may have meant a total renewal in your life and in your heart. If so, mission accomplished. And I thank God for that. If not, I hope that at least it has been useful to you for your own good, or for the good of someone you know. I firmly believe that the Lord has the power to heal and regenerate hearts, and I am firmly persuaded that it happened to you too.

Today you start a new life, because you have a brand-new heart. You are now a new creature, with a new heart, and a new purpose, that you have to fight to preserve, until the day you surrender yourself from the heart and for good to the person for whom you have recovered your virginity. Because life´s purpose is love and surrender.

No one may realize that your life has changed, your daily life may not change about anything in particular, but you and the Lord know that it is so, because the miracle has happened in your heart. And that's where the greatest victories take place. Those victories which nobody sees, the ones that change the world. Your heart has become a paradise, a hidden treasure, a heart of flesh, whole, pure, regenerated and renewed. It beats again strongly, filling you with a new life.

If all this is true, you will have three very beautiful and important consequences for your life: hope, joy and peace.

Hope, because you have discovered that the power of God is greater than any power in the world, and that good overcomes evil; that nothing is impossible for God, and that there is nothing that He cannot forgive, heal and restore. For all that we have hope.

Joy, because it is the fruit of a heart healed and freed by God. A heart looked at and loved with mercy. The joy that springs from the miracle of transformation that God has done in your life; the joy that comes from your new path, always towards greater fullness.

Peace, because your heart is now reconciled, with your past, with yourself and with others. Peace, because you have discovered that God is the Lord of the universe, and that everything contributes to his plan of love, because he is capable of making good come out from evil. It is possible that the restlessness of your heart vanishes now and that you recover the peace that perhaps you had lost through sin.

And I want to end by telling you that you are brave:

Brave for wanting to live chastity and virginity in a world where it is not easy and you choose to swim against the tide.

Brave for daring to face the mistakes of the past and face them, for daring to return to them and also to leave them behind.

Brave for letting God in your life and giving him all your misery, and for daring to take this step of recovering your virginity and committing again to the Lord, willing to live by his will, even if it is not easy.

And I am sure that today, in heaven, they´re throwing a party; because the power of God triumphs over the weakness of the creature, and also because of the fact that God´s mercy has once again annihilated the power of evil. And I am sure that today, as always, the words of Jesus resonate again:

«And he who sat on the throne said: "Look, I make all things new". And he said: "Put it in the book; for these words are certain and true". And he said: "It is done. I am the Alpha and the Omega, the beginning and the end. I will give freely from the source of the water of life to those in need. He who overcomes will inherit this; I will be God for him, and he shall be my son"» (Ap 21, 5 – 7).

This is for your partner if has kept the virginity for you

I want to address a few words to you, who have saved your virginity for your future husband or wife, and that you are now with someone who lost their virginity. This situation can be very difficult for you, and sometimes create problems for you: jealousy, sadness, fear for the future... I have talked to many people who, just like you, have remained a virgin and are now going out with someone who lost their virginity; some of those people feel sadness, because they feel that their boyfriend or girlfriend has given to another what was his or her responsibility, and they feel that, in some way, their current partner should apologize for having lost their virginity and not having preserved it for them. That is true in a way, and it is something that you may have to talk through, because it may be healing for both of you that he or she apologizes for not having saved it for you. But you should also realize that when your partner slept with other people, perhaps they did it unconsciously, or without giving it the meaning that now they give to relationships; maybe they did it by mistake, or without realizing the consequences that would have on their life and on their relationship with you. If he or she wants to live chastity, I assure you they are the ones suffering the most since somehow, they would like to have kept that for you. You shouldn´t think that having had sex with another person made them reach a greater intimacy than what they might reach with you. It is true that sexuality has to be a surrender, but it is also true that surrender is not just sexual. And I assure you that the love and intimacy they have with you, through chastity, are much more beautiful and profound than anything they have ever lived before with anyone else.

First of all believe in the power of God, which can regenerate the heart of your boyfriend or girlfriend and make it virginal again for you. If it had not been by the grace of God and by his mercy, you might have done the same; or maybe even worse things. You are for your boyfriend or girlfriend an image of God's merciful gaze, which not only does not face or condemn, but restores and regenerates the heart. Through your chaste look, God can return purity to the heart of your boyfriend or girlfriend. Praise him as Christ welcomed men after mankind departed from God's way; welcome your partner as the father welcomed his son, hugging him and covering him with kisses, dressing him with the best robe, the ring of the new alliance, the sandals of innocence; welcome him and surrender to him or her, as Christ gave himself up for his wife, the Church, to make her holy and immaculate. So that your boyfriend or girlfriend can see what Paul says: «Love is patient, is kind, It does not envy, it does not boast, it is not proud. It does not dishonor others, it is not self-seeking, it is not easily angered, it keeps no record of wrongs. Love does not delight in evil but rejoices with the truth. It always protects, always trusts, always hopes, always perseveres. Love never passes» (1 Cor 13, 4 – 8).

I know this is difficult, because we are human, and our gaze is not like God's. That your boyfriend or girlfriend is reading this book is the perfect occasion for you to talk about those issues that are pending that may be hurting you. It may be hard, but also a very important exercise, so those wounds can heal, so that your relationship can reach the depth to which it is called. This takes time, it even maybe after marriage when such wounds can heal, since only in marriage will total surrender take place even sexually. Be patient, believe in the power of God, love with all your might and do not be afraid to talk about all possible issues thing with your partner, because

God can bring out good out of it all. Courage! The road ahead is unique and beautiful.

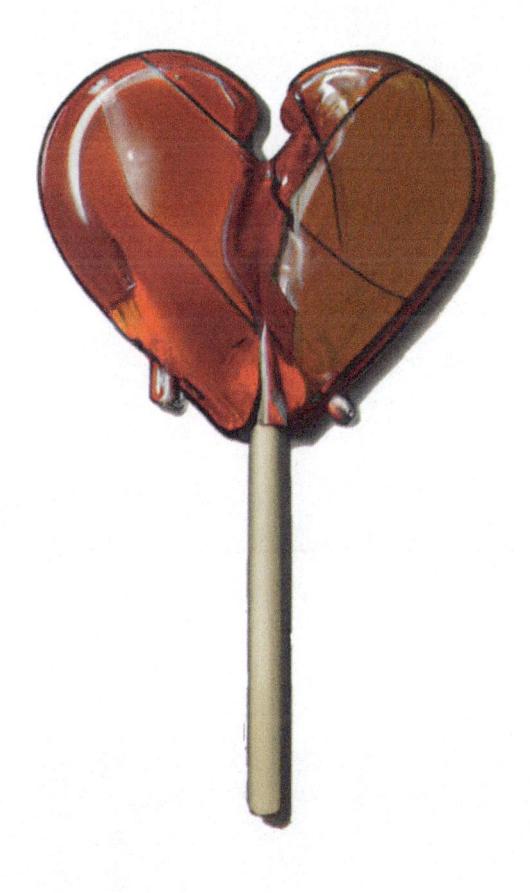